Brett Younger is a keen observer of the human condition. Mixing a sense of humor with the timing of a great storyteller, he reminds us that there are lessons to be learned about us as human beings, about God, and about the relationship between the divine and humanity. Most of all, Brett's writings should cause us all to say that we too just want to be a Christian.

—Michael Chittum
Executive Director, National Association of
Congregational Christian Churches

Many people of faith feel almost stricken in these days: how in the world do we stay engaged, let alone in dialogue, with one another? How do we speak up and out, with love and respect? Brett Younger has found a way, and in this wonderful book, he shows us what it looks like. Pay attention to the ordinary scenes unfolding around you. Find the hilarity and the heartbreak; they go hand in hand. Write it all down, sparing no one--least of all, yourself. And trust that telling the truth is holy, essential work. This is a book that will give you courage to get up in the morning.

—Anna Carter Florence
Peter Marshall Professor of Preaching
Columbia Theological Seminary, Decatur, Georgia

Brett Younger is a voice of joy and sanity in a world of judgment and division. His collection of essays will make you think, laugh, pray, and ponder. Most of all, it will leave you lighter and brighter. Thank you for this much needed gift of hope and laughter!

—Susan Sparks
Senior Pastor, Madison Avenue Baptist Church, New York City
Author of *Preaching Punchlines: The Ten Commandments of Comedy*

Brett Younger is the funniest pastor I know. And I know a lot of pastors, although clearly not the right ones. If you're serious about the faith but not somber in how you talk about it, Brett could be your favorite pastor. And if you don't want to read a book of sermons, pick up this collection instead; it's got more Bible truth than seven out of ten sermons.

—Mark Wingfield
Associate pastor, Wilshire Baptist Church
Baptist News Global columnist

Smyth & Helwys Publishing, Inc.
6316 Peake Road
Macon, Georgia 31210-3960
1-800-747-3016

All photographs, unless otherwise noted, are courtesy of the author.

Library of Congress Cataloging-in-Publication Data

Names: Younger, Brett, 1961- author.
Title: Funny when you think about it : serious reflections on faith / by
    Brett Younger.
Description: Macon, GA : Smyth & Helwys Publishing, 2020.
Identifiers: LCCN 2019029870 (print) | LCCN 2019029871 (ebook) | ISBN
    9781641731638 (paperback) | ISBN 9781641731645 (epub)
Subjects: LCSH: Christian life. | Theology.
Classification: LCC BV4510.3 .Y68 2019 (print) | LCC BV4510.3 (ebook) |
    DDC 277.3/083--dc23
LC record available at https://lccn.loc.gov/2019029870
LC ebook record available at https://lccn.loc.gov/2019029871

Funny When You Think About It

SERIOUS REFLECTIONS ON FAITH

Brett Younger

Also by Brett Younger

Living with Stress: Nurturing Joy in a Tension-filled World
(with Carol Younger)

Mark: Finding Ourselves in the Story
(with Carol Younger)

Spirituality: Finding Your Way

Time for Supper: Invitations to Christ's Table

Who Moved My Pulpit? A Hilarious Look at Ministerial Life

To Carol,
who makes me think

Contents

Introduction

Writing for Baptist News Global is a great job. The salary is not much, and there are no retirement or health benefits, but I get to work at home and I almost never see my boss. This job forces me to pay attention. Once a month I get to ask, "What's happening that people want to read about?"

I carry a composition book everywhere and hope something interesting will happen. While other church staff members want the annual pancake race to go off without a hitch, I, who have a column due, hope something goes awry. For example, when Mary and Joseph showed up at our church's meal with the homeless on a cold night in December, I was as disappointed as Joseph to learn that Mary was there with Kevin. Also, I would never have attended the hot dog eating contest at Coney Island without knowing my disgust would become fodder for a column.

I pay more attention and have a better perspective when I view the world as potential material for columns. When Van Morrison's *Greatest Hits* gets stuck in the CD player, it is a colorful detail instead of an irritant. When I find a granola bar in my pocket, it becomes part of a story. When Amy Poehler takes a seat two tables away at the restaurant, I start noting what everyone is eating.

Writing helps me enjoy things I would not otherwise enjoy. No one asked me to speak at Carroll Spinney's retirement, but I got to write the speech I would have given, lamenting the fact that Big Bird and Oscar's voice would never be the same. I will not be invited to do a set at Manhattan's Comedy Cellar, but I have a routine ready if I am.

Writing a column while serving on a seminary faculty made me consider what serving on a seminary faculty should mean. When my school increased its number of online classes, I began writing a complaint and then was surprised when it turned into a thank-you note to my former professors. When gathering info for a column about race and seminary education, I had a chance to talk with three African American preaching students. When I was not invited to be the graduation speaker, I had a reason to write a speech anyway. When I was dealing with grief over leaving my seminary, I had an excuse to list the things I would miss—and the things I would not.

For the five months that we lived in Santiago, Chile, writing columns felt like writing home. When I got lost, I thought, "This will read like it was more fun than it is." When I was in a grocery store unable to come up with the Spanish word for salad dressing, I asked myself, "Is this amusing?" When I was mistaken for an Australian, I was excited to know that I could tell my readers someone thought I was an Aussie. When I heard the story of a Catholic priest falling in love, my reaction was, "I get to tell this amazing story of a Catholic priest falling in love." When I realized that being in South America turned everything I had learned about missions on its head, I needed to write about it.

Later, a friend asked, "Why are you moving from Atlanta to Brooklyn?" I said, "We're trying something different." He responded, "I think you overshot." On the days when it felt like we overshot, writing a column was cheaper than counseling. Many Baptist News readers understand why I miss Waffle House and do not quite get bagels, egg creams, and lacrosse. Writing about your new home makes it feel more like home.

Church is more interesting, too, if you write about it. When I overheard an usher complain about someone drinking coffee in the sanctuary, I got to research the religious implications of caffeine. I pay more attention to Reformation Day if I am writing 700 words about it. Opinion writing led me to reflect on Justin Bieber's baptism. When I first heard the term "virtual church," it sounded silly, so I wrote a column that amused old people. I have poked fun at Calvinism, Second Coming goofiness, and *The American Patriot's Bible.* I wrote a column mocking people who lead marriage retreats right after my wife, Carol, and I led a marriage retreat.

Writing a column makes me think deeper thoughts about politics. I have discovered that more people are likely to read a column if it has Donald Trump's name in the title. The title "Donald Trump Stole My Old Church" led to 73,000 shares and two radio interviews. When Paul Ryan forced the House chaplain to resign, I was sad but also thought, "That's strange enough to write about." Listening to people twist Scripture for political reasons—as in the case of *Masterpiece Cakeshop v. Colorado Civil Rights Commission*—made me think about how I twist Scripture for political reasons. When a patriot handed me a tiny American flag, it felt like I was being handed a writing assignment.

I have better, clearer childhood memories because I write for baptist-news.com. When I met my eighth grade social studies teacher for coffee, I appreciated the chance to tell my readers how my old friends Goony and Peachy are doing. Remembering a silly childhood debate—whether flight or invisibility would be the better superpower—sparked genuine reflection. When I write about racism in 1960s Mississippi, I become more determined to write for change. When my youth minister told us not to date Methodists in 1974, it was not funny, but now it is.

I am grateful to David Wilkinson at Baptist News Global for inviting me to write and to Keith Gammons, publisher, and Leslie Andres, editor, at Smyth & Helwys for putting these columns together into a collection.

When I saw a "Before I die" wall in Asheville, North Carolina, I took photos of what people had written. Before I die I want to . . . "Swim in a pool of golden retriever puppies. Do a cartwheel. Straddle the international dateline. Fall in love. Own a llama farm." I should have added, "Before I die I want to write a book on the marvelous confluence of faith and just about everything else."

Many of the subjects in these columns are not amusing—racism, gun violence, suicide—but tragedy and comedy can be two sides of the same coin. There's a reason we get more of our news from Stephen Colbert than from Lester Holt. Hope is when tragedy leaves a space for comedy. I hope this book reminds you that it really is funny when you think about it.

Everyday Theology

Here are your inspirational clichés for today (October 22, 2019)

"This is the day that the Lord has made!" declares the psalmist. "Let us rejoice and be glad in it!!" (Psalm 118:24, punctuation mine!).

The Lord made this beautiful day. The sun is inviting you to come outside and rejoice. The warmth of this day will make you feel warm inside.

Or it is cold and rainy. The Lord made this dismal day. The dreariness of this day is inviting you to stay inside, because you have to look through the rain to see the rainbow. Or you should go outside because life is not about waiting for the storm to pass, but learning to dance in the rain.

You got out of bed this morning, which would be a big deal if you could not get out of bed. If you are reading these inspirational thoughts while still in bed, that's fine, too. Rest in the glory of this awesome day.

If you are a person who begins each day with inspirational thoughts, then you already know that this is the day that the Lord has made. If you are surprised to learn this, then you need to listen to the robins greet the morning. Welcome the day with your own song of joy. Hear the coffee shouting, "Wake up!" Be caffeinated with excitement. Look at the flower poking through the sidewalk. Be persistent like that daisy.

The psalmist is warning you: "This is the day that the Lord has made! Let us rejoice and be glad in it!" If you are not paying attention, then you might forget who made this day and be bored in it.

Psalm 118 was written for the king of Israel's victorious return from battle, but for us it is a big yellow smiley face, "Have a nice day!" This psalm can change your morning, your day, and you! Let this song fill you with cheerfulness.

If you think God has closed a door, then start looking for the window God has opened. Maybe God has closed a door because you have the wrong address. Or God wants you to kick down the door.

Have a blessed day, because today is the first day of the rest of your life. Yesterday is history, tomorrow a mystery, and today a gift. That is why we call it the present.

Keep calm and carry on. Let go and let God. Take a break. Put on the brakes.

Everything happens for a reason, except for unreasonable things. What does not kill you makes you stronger, except for really bad stuff. Cleanliness is next to godliness, which is unfair to those without access to running water. But as it says nowhere in the Bible, God never gives you more than you can handle.

God works in mysterious ways and helps those who help themselves. Life is what happens while you are busy making other plans, but life is 10 percent what happens to you and 90 percent how you react to it.

Dream as if you will live forever. Live every day like it is your last. Treat everyone as if this were their last day.

If life gives you lemons, make lemonade, because it takes more muscles to frown than it does to smile.

You miss 100 percent of the shots you do not take, so shoot for the moon. Even if you miss, you will land among the stars, even though this does not seem scientifically accurate.

Live. Laugh. Love. It is not the number of breaths we take, but the number of moments that take our breath away before we get right back to breathing normally.

Sing like no one is listening. Love like you have never been hurt. Dance like the people who are watching think you are a good dancer.

Do not feel sad if you are reading these inspirational thoughts just before going to sleep and you did not spend the day thinking about this being the day that the Lord has made and being glad in it. Tomorrow will also be a day that the Lord will make. You can rejoice and be glad in it tomorrow.

Waking up to routine and finding ourselves surprised (June 15, 2017)

The alarm goes off long before you want it to. The snooze button is not worth it, but it is tempting. You have to get to work. Or you have to get to work at home. Or you have learned that retirement is work.

The crowd going to work does not eat a healthy breakfast. A granola bar in your pocket. A chicken biscuit at a drive-through. Some of us have eaten fruit roll-ups for breakfast.

You glance at the headlines on your phone. You get more of your news from Stephen Colbert than Lester Holt.

You get to the office and are greeted by a coworker who is way too cheerful. You open your email and are reminded that you should not open your email first thing. You still have emails you did not want to deal with yesterday, and now you have new emails and still no desire to deal with them.

You are probably going to end up eating lunch at your desk again. You are doing the same things you did yesterday and the day before that. You are going to do the same things tomorrow and the day after that. It is Groundhog Day all over again.

You plan to get home as soon as possible, put on your pajamas way too early, and watch *House of Cards*. You will watch one more episode than you should of Frank and Claire destroying helpless people.

Our lives are predictable, which can be dull, but that is not all bad. We no longer spend time hoping someone important will see how great we are and make our lives perfect.

We are used to the way things are. We know the people we live with, and how to keep them from driving us crazy. We have figured out the easiest way to get wherever we have to go. We know which restaurants work for us. We know which podcasts we listen to. We know which websites we frequent. Familiar can be comfortable, like putting on your pajamas at 7:00.

We know who we are at work. We know most people's names. We are fairly friendly.

We are people who get angry about politics but don't do much about it.

We know how we respond when homeless people ask for money. We have decided that it is not an efficient way to help, so we have gotten used to walking by.

We know who we are around children. Maybe we are people who do not know names but like calling children "Bud" and "Honey."

The idea that something life-changing could happen does not enter our minds. We are too old to fall in love, too tired to feel too excited, and too reasonable to do much that is unreasonable.

But there are moments in the middle of a regular day when something (or someone) stirs our soul and opens our eyes.

You are having a normal morning when you look across the breakfast table, see someone you love, and remember why you love them.

You are ignoring the crowd crossing the street when God's children start shining like the sun.

You have a moment when you become a person who has conversations with homeless people: "Have you lived here all your life?"

You are in a dull meeting when you have an uninvited thought and say, "I have an idea that could make a real difference."

You ask a coworker, "How are your children?" and listen carefully for the answer.

You find yourself on the floor playing with a child. You are not sure how you got to the floor, but you are happy to be there.

You read the news and decide it is not enough to think right. You have to resist. You join a group to fight for what you believe.

You read a column that is trying hard to be inspiring when you realize what you need to write.

You feel alive for just a moment. The moment passes so quickly, you wonder if it is real.

These are the closing lines of Mary Oliver's "When Death Comes":

When it's over, I don't want to wonder
if I have made of my life something particular, and real.
I don't want to find myself sighing and frightened, or full of argument.
I don't want to end up simply having visited this world.

We need to wake up to those moments when we are more than visitors to our own lives.

Finding a Bible that fits (March 22, 2011)

I wandered into the Bible section at a Borders bookstore going-out-of-business sale and thought, "I need more choices." Fortunately, the publishers are looking out for me. On Ash Wednesday, new translations of the New International Version (the most popular evangelical version) and the New American Bible (the official Catholic version) were released.

Bible sellers understand that we need updated versions because outdated words get in the way, Hebrew and Greek professors get smarter, and Indiana Jones keeps finding old scraps of Scripture.

One change in the NIV replaces "booty" with "spoils of war." This is a prudent decision.

Another change is Isaiah 7:14, which now says, "Look, the young woman shall be with child and bear a son and shall name him Immanuel." The earlier version used "virgin" instead of "young woman." The translators hope no one notices until December.

This latest NIV has dropped some gender-neutral language that publishers flirted with in a 2005 version; they backed off because of criticism by conservatives. We were "human beings" for six years, but we are "mankind" again.

I am all for removing superfluous references to booty and virgins, but you have to wonder how updated we need to be. "Thees" and "thous" becoming "yous" and "y'alls" is great, but that may not be the real issue.

The novelty Bible industry is there for anyone still carrying the Gideon Bible they took from the Hampton Inn. Novelty Bibles dress up Holy Scripture in fashionable ways. The dozens of niche-marketed Bibles include *The Hope for Today Bible* (featuring notes and encouragement from Joel and Victoria Osteen), *The Charles F. Stanley Life Principles Bible*, *The Golfer's Bible*, *The Jogger's Bible*, and *The Green Bible* (a "green letter edition" with a thousand verses highlighted). Only a cynical person would see these as ploys to sell Bibles to eager proof-texters.

The *American Patriot's Bible* comes in camouflage. A defense of the Second Amendment is found in Exodus, the Declaration of Independence appears in the middle of Joshua, and an overview of World War II is given in First Timothy. Each Gospel opens with a picture of soldiers struggling to raise a flag under the words "In God We Trust," but no footnotes are wasted explaining how beating swords into plowshares can be considered patriotic in a country where half of our taxes go to military spending.

Maybe what we want is not more translators but more aggressive editors. The Bible is filled with sections we could do without.

What about a *Less Peculiar Bible*? In this sensible version, the oddest rules are gone. Do we really need to break a cow's neck at the sight of an unsolved murder (Deut 21:1-6)? What about the prohibitions on two kinds of material in the same garment (Lev 19:19)? If I get into a fight and my wife inadvertently grabs the privates of my opponent, I do not want to have to cut off her hand (Deut 25:11-12). It may even be time to let go of capital punishment for breaking the Sabbath (Exod 31:14).

What about a *Wealthy Americans Bible*? In this sensitive-to-the-rich version, the last judgment story about the sheep and goats, the parable of the rich man and Lazarus, and that section in Acts where the early church sounds like a bunch of communists are out. Who wouldn't want a Bible where Jesus tells the rich young ruler that he is fine just the way he is? Removing 3,000 verses on caring for the poor makes this an ultra-thin version.

With all the advancements in self-publishing, we cannot be far from being able to order a personalized Bible. I would love to give my mother a Bible in which the Old Testament polygamists are monogamous, Jesus changes the water into Welch's grape juice, and Song of Solomon is nowhere to be found.

One of Mark Twain's best-known quotations is, "It's not the parts of the Bible that I don't understand that bother me; it's the parts that I do understand."

We are tempted to live a careful faith, keep six of the Ten Commandments, go to church twice a month, give money we do not need, offer some grace and more judgment, and affirm the parts of the Bible with which we already agree, but God calls us to more.

The Bible is older, smarter, and better than we are. We do not need to find the Bible that suits us. We need to live pursuing the hard truth.

Counting the days (April 11, 2011)

When I was in the seventh grade, a white-suited evangelist guaranteed that Jesus would be back in less than five years. Every thirteen-year-old boy at church that night had the same thought: "I will never get to have sex."

Another evangelist is making the news frightening teenage boys. Rev. Harold Camping, president of the Family Radio Christian Network, is predicting that the rapture will take place on May 21. He says that approximately three percent of the world's population will be taken into heaven. Doesn't that seem low? You and I may not be making the trip.

The May 21 guarantee has been displayed on buses, benches, and billboards. Five Family Radio RVs covered with reflective lettering are traveling around the country declaring that Judgment Day is less than two weeks after Mother's Day.

The prophetic proof that May 21 is the day to end all days is rock solid. According to Camping, the number five equals "atonement," the number ten equals "completeness," and the number seventeen equals "heaven." Pay attention or you may get lost. Christ died on the cross on April 1, AD 33. The time between April 1, 33, and April 1, 2011, is 1,978 years.

Are you still with us? If 1,978 is multiplied by 365.2422 days (the number of days in a solar year, not to be confused with the lunar year), the result is 722,449. The time between April 1 and May 21 is 51 days. (Don't get too far ahead!) When you add 51 to 722,449, you get 722,500. Then, multiply $(5 \times 10 \times 17)^2$ (that is, [atonement x completeness x heaven]^2) also equals 722,500.

Aren't you embarrassed that you didn't think of this? Camping concludes that 5x10x17 is telling us a "story from the time Christ made payment for our sins until we're completely saved."

As if that's not enough proof—and what kind of heretic would need more evidence?—May 21, 2011, is 7,000 years to the day since the first raindrops fell to start Noah's flood. How could it be more obvious? The logic is indisputable.

Rev. Camping is not just making stuff up. He is a successful self-published author of *Time Has an End* (2005), *We Are Almost There!* (2008), *The End of the World Is Almost Here!* (2009), and *God Gives Another Infallible Proof that Assures the Rapture Will Occur May 21, 2011* (2009). Camping writes, "I know it's absolutely true because the Bible is always absolutely true." How could anyone argue with that?

Some doubters condescendingly note that Jesus said no one would know when the end is near. Cynics also love to point out that in his 1992 book *1994?* Camping predicted that the end would come on September 4, 1994. He later correctly pointed out that he had made a mathematical error. Enough said.

Admittedly, there is a history of failed predictions that could be considered embarrassing. In the year 1000, a flurry of prophetic forecasts led many Christians to expect Jesus soon. William Miller predicted that the Second Coming would take place in 1843. His followers, the Seventh Day Adventists, have since adjusted their schedule. Charles Taze Russell, founder of the Jehovah's Witnesses, predicted the apocalypse would be in 1914. They also have postponed the end of the world.

The best-selling religious book of the 1970s was Hal Lindsey's *The Late Great Planet Earth*. The author predicted that Jesus would return within a few years. The profits from the book paid for a mansion that took three years to build. Then, as the year 2000 approached, people began finding references to Y2K in the book of Revelation. The *Left Behind* series made huge money even though the kid from *Growing Pains* starred in the movie version.

While many so-called Christian scholars are claiming that Camping is similarly mistaken, let's not be too hasty. What if the good reverend is right? If Harold's calculations are correct, won't you feel goofy if you ignore him? I have decided not to take chances.

Just in case May 21 is the end, I am not going to be watching my cholesterol on May 20. I will not be mowing my lawn, cleaning my refrigerator, or doing the laundry. My doctor has been after me to get a colonoscopy. I have scheduled it for June.

What would it hurt to treat May 20 like a holy day? Pray. Read a psalm. Read a poem. Sing. Dance. Give something away. Listen to the people you love. Tell them how much they mean to you. Forgive old grudges.

Encourage worried thirteen-year-old boys that everything will be fine—no matter what.

There is something to be said for living every day as if it were your last because someday you'll be right. And if God shows up, how great will that be?

I had no choice but to write this column (July 19, 2013)

Smilin' John Calvin was born in France in 1509. Educated as a lawyer, John found jurisprudence too free-wheeling, so he switched his affection to the church.

During his ministry in Geneva, Calvin preached more than 2,000 sermons. His sermons lasted over an hour and he did not use notes. Those listening did not take notes either, but they were expected to pay attention. In 1547, a man who left during the sermon was imprisoned.

Calvin proposed to one woman on the condition that she learn French, but he broke that off and graciously—romantic that he was—wrote that he would never think of marrying her "unless the Lord had entirely bereft me of my wits." Later that same year he married Idelette de Bure, a widow whose first husband was—imagine the scandal—an Anabaptist.

Smilin' Jack

Titian (?–1576). *Portrait of Jean Calvin*. Oil on canvas. (Credit: Wikimedia, PD-old)

Calvin was sick for much of his life, suffering from tuberculosis, heart problems, malaria, and kidney stones. According to one source, Calvin passed a stone the size of a chestnut. This might explain his crankiness.

Not-so-silent Cal did not, for instance, care for Jewish people: "Their rotten and unbending stiffneckedness deserves that they be oppressed unendingly and without measure or end and that they die in their misery without the pity of anyone."

Calvin also did not care for Michael Servetus, a Protestant theologian who disagreed with Calvin on the doctrine of the Trinity. When Servetus came to Geneva to talk about their differences, he was sentenced to burning at the stake. Calvin, softy that he was, suggested that he simply be beheaded, but leniency only goes so far.

How could the New Calvinists not fall in love with the prophet of doom who wrote, "All things being at God's disposal, and the decision of salvation or death belonging to him, he orders all things by his counsel and decree in such a manner, that some men are born devoted from the womb to certain death, that his name may be glorified in their destruction"?

Southern Baptists are gushing over this poet of predestination. The young, restless, and reformed are pushing for a straightforward theology that doesn't bother with questions.

Frank Page, president and chief executive officer of the SBC Executive Committee and a self-described "non-Calvinist," is so worried about Calvin's groupies that he formed "The Advisory Team on Calvinism" (which looks great on a T-shirt) to ease tensions between the chosen and the choosing.

The team's seven-page report, "Truth, Trust and Testimony in a Time of Tension," laid out the differences. Interestingly, the New Calvinists are not pushing for Calvin's views on church/state, church governance, or infant baptism.

Some Baptist moderates are amused that Southern Baptists are now looking for ways, according to Steve Lemke, provost at New Orleans Baptist Theological Seminary (who sounds so 1980 when he talks about including everybody), to seek balance, sensitivity, and an openness to divergent viewpoints.

The news that a schism would be a problem for a denomination in decline is a little late. The idea of staying together and disagreeing may have made sense thirty years ago, but it is not likely to work this time. Calvinists are not like terrorists; you can reason with terrorists.

The rising popularity of Calvinism has to be attributed to its cool TULIP acronym. The five points of Calvinism are:

T—Total Depravity. All of us are really, really, *really* bad. Adolf Hitler, Joseph Stalin, and Britney Spears bad. Mother Teresa, on the other hand, is bad like Kim Kardashian.

U—Unconditional Election. Calvinist scoreboards display the final score at the beginning of the game. John Edwards, Paris Hilton, and Charlie Sheen never had a chance. A Calvinist in a car accident can only lament, "I'm glad that's over."

L—Limited Atonement. Jesus died not for the world (no more John 3:16 bumper stickers) but for the elect. A hyper-Calvinist is not a Presbyterian drinking Mountain Dew but one who recognizes that God orders, decrees, and determines but does not invite.

I—Irresistible Grace. God brings the elect to salvation through an internal call that they are powerless to resist. Real Calvinists are confused by buffets and have trouble with multiple-choice questions.

P—Perseverance of the Saints. Once in, always in. Calvinists don't sign up for dating services. They just wait for the call.

Most of the Calvinists I know seem like Universalists with anger issues. I would much rather follow Calvin and Hobbes than John Calvin, but maybe God made me that way.

Your commute as a spiritual discipline (April 14, 2016)

My morning commute reminds me that I am not the Christian I should be. I drive nine miles to my job—two miles of neighborhood, three miles of suburban commerce, and four miles of houses close enough to Atlanta that we cannot afford them. The trip takes about twenty-five minutes, which is considered next door in Atlanta. (I tried the interstate once. After an hour, I vowed not to make that mistake again.)

I pass train tracks, two tiny cemeteries, and what may be the only full-service gas station in the city. Sometimes I drive through McDonald's. I have decided that the breakfast burrito is, sadly, the best I can do. I tried to get them to start offering iced decaf coffee by ordering it five days in a row, but they just grew irritated.

I go by four churches. They have helpful information on their marquees—"Join us for worship at 11 on Sunday"—but I keep hoping for "Choose the Bread of Life or you are toast."

I have made this trip more than a thousand times. If I leave home at 7:00, I am in danger of stopping at every other house behind a school bus.

If I leave at 7:15, I may get stuck in front of Tucker High School, where the students move slowly across the street. When I use the navigation app Waze to avoid traffic, I drive by retirees walking their dogs. I try to look like I am not cutting through their neighborhood to take two minutes off my commute.

When two lanes merge into one, I strain to think good things about the drivers who cut to the front of the line. Perhaps they are all rushing to the hospital to deliver babies. I find it easier to exercise patience since my horn stopped working two years ago.

Sometimes I listen to sports talk on 680 The Fan:

"Which happens first—the Falcons win the Super Bowl, the Braves win the World Series, or Tyler Perry wins an Academy Award?"

"Could the Oscar be for costume design?"

"Would you rather your child lose a toe or become an Alabama fan?"

"Which toe?"

I have not found the radio station that plays the music I love. The only singer I recognize on most stations is Adele. The country stations do not work for me because I do not go to honky-tonks nearly as often as you might think. There is no all-Bruce-Springsteen-all-the-time station.

I drive a 1998 Ford Escort that was totaled a year ago when a driver talking on a cell phone ran into me. The CD player has not worked in five years. Van Morrison's *Greatest Hits* is stuck in there. Early each May, I get the air conditioner fixed. I have cold air until the middle of August.

When I am feeling smart, I turn to the news on NPR. I try to remain interested when they discuss the major exports of Tunisia, but I do not know where Tunisia is.

For the last few years, I have been listening to podcasts. *10% Happier* is about meditation, which is a challenge when driving in Atlanta. *NPR Politics* has been depressing since the presidential campaigns have started again. *On Being*, an amazing discussion of faith, is the podcast most easily quoted in sermons. I usually love *Radiolab*, but a recent episode on South Korean pop stars suggests I may not be their target audience. I listen to Garrison Keillor's news from Lake Wobegon, "where the women are strong, the men are good-looking, and the children are above average."

When I call Carol on my way home, she knows I am killing time and says sweet things like "I'll be glad to talk when you get home." When I call my parents, they "don't want to talk too long because it's long distance."

Lately I have been driving in silence. I notice more when the car is quiet. I wave at the walker who goes backward up the hill near our house. I do not know the names of the flowers, but I look for the dark red and white ones.

Sometimes I pray. On the way to work, I pray that I will remember that God will be with me through the day. I cannot close my eyes, so I pray for the students crossing against the light. I notice the other drivers—signs that God is as present on Georgia State Highway 29 as at the seminary to which I'm driving. On the way home, I apologize for the ways I have forgotten that God was with me.

We are more ourselves when driving alone than at almost any other time. Would we want to be friends with the person we are when drive? Are we following Christ when we are heading to work?

What we do in the car may not sound like a test of faith, but it is an opportunity for faith. For a long time, I did not expect much from myself on my commute, but I am learning.

A few words against faith (August 7, 2015)

I've about had it with faith. When Paul says, "And now faith, hope, and love abide, these three" (1 Cor 13:13), I hope the order is alphabetical.

I am fine with hope—*Shawshank Redemption* kind of hope. Andy Dufresne writes, "Remember, Red, hope is a good thing, maybe the best of things, and no good thing ever dies."

I am good with love—*Princess Bride* kind of love. Westley asks, "I told you I would always come for you. Why didn't you wait for me?" Buttercup responds, "Well . . . you were dead." Westley replies, "Death cannot stop true love. All it can do is delay it for a while."

I am done with faith—*Miracle on 34th Street* kind of faith. Fred the lawyer argues, "Faith is believing when common sense tells you not to."

Faith is the shaky one, but it has won the day. Googling "Christian hope" leads to about 392,000 results, "Christian love" to 570,000, and "Christian faith" to 11,300,000. The prevailing view is that Christianity is a set of ideas.

Some churches suggest faith is believing things that are not true. I was taught that faith says, "Everything works for good," "God doesn't put more on us than we can handle," and "It does not make sense to you or me or any thinking scientist, but the world is 6,000 years old." For some, faith is thinking that, though it seems cruel, God is keeping your grandmother alive in the nursing home for years after she wants to go. For some, faith is believing that God gives leukemia to a seven-year-old so she can sing in the heavenly choir. Some think that those who have the most faith are the ones who argue the loudest that the Christian faith is right and everyone else's faith is wrong.

Somehow when Jesus said, "Come, follow me," would-be followers heard, "Come, write creeds about what everyone has to think." The Christian faith is reduced to opinions about the Trinity, the Bible, the church, sin, and salvation. Stingy orthodoxy chokes the hope and love with which the story started. Some of the least loving people win Bible trivia. Some of the least hopeful people say the Apostles' Creed without peeking at the order of worship.

The church too often measures not by heart and soul but by conformity of thought. What passes for faith trumps hope and love. The church tells its members, "You have to believe these ten ideas to be a Christian." Then a fifteen-year-old takes tenth-grade biology and has to choose between science and faith.

For many, accepting easy answers and skipping hard questions does not work. Giving themselves to ideas that are less than the best ideas feels like wearing someone else's wooden shoes. They cannot give their hearts to what their minds cannot accept. They cannot love a God they do not really believe in.

So the restless ones want a broader faith, more education, and better ideas. They work to correct the answers they have been given. They make room for everything that is true. They do faith with a pencil and eraser in a loose-leaf notebook (or with an open computer file for which you do not get to hit "save"). They look for the smallest number of opinions they can hold and still be Christian.

The difficulty with putting our ultimate trust in more open-minded theology is that Paul argues not for a wider faith as "the greatest of these," but for "love." When Jesus was asked for the greatest commandment, he went with "Love God" and "Love your neighbor."

The questions are still bigger than our biggest ideas. Even the broadest faith does not give the answers we want. Why is there so much suffering? What is the relationship of Christianity to other religions? What about eternity? The questions are beyond our ability to answer. The God of mystery does not make us feel smart. We cannot trust a faith that we can explain, but we can hope beyond our explanations.

We can put our faith not in refining our ideas about God but in God. We can understand Christianity not as a set of beliefs but as the way of life revealed in Jesus. We can live with hope and love like Jesus. We can live with faith in the wild hope and deep love of God.

Sins I could have committed, but I was on the other team (September 14, 2017)

The teachers never checked the area between the gym and the cafeteria—the perfect place for high-stakes penny pitching. Fifth-grade boys lined up during recess and threw pennies at a brick wall. Whoever's penny stayed closest to the wall won all of the pennies. This was the most fun anyone had ever had, but I knew it was gambling.

I took a pocketful of pennies one day just in case I succumbed to temptation, but I was not like most children. I was afraid that if I threw a penny against the gym wall, I would end up destitute in Las Vegas, sitting on the sidewalk begging for money to lose at the blackjack table. My refusal looked like following rules, but it was really about being loyal to the team. My team was made up of people who did not gamble. The reason I have never ever, not once, bought a lottery ticket is that I was taught, "You're better than that." "You're better than that" is not far from "You're better than them."

One Saturday afternoon, our church softball team defeated some Baptist church that had not won the associational crown three years in a row. My friend Jeff saw a friend two fields over playing a pick-up game, so the two of us went to join in. Their cooler was different from the Baptist coolers to which I had grown accustomed. Theirs was filled with Miller High Life. The scene was a beer commercial: people playing ball, laughing in the sun, dropping a cold one. Jeff was downing his second, so he was not going to tell. No one would ever know. I could taste the High Life! But I was afraid that if I took a sip, I would wake up on skid row with an unkempt beard. I stayed sober because I was on the other team. I had my first drink of wine—I know how provincial this makes me sound—at an Episcopal Communion service when I was thirty years old.

When I was in high school, a group decided to go to a Bruce Springsteen concert and—this is the surprising part—I was invited. I was not invited by my church friends. Someone in Algebra II, who showed signs of being an atheist, invited me. I heard stories about marijuana smoke drifting through the arena at rock concerts. It would be in the very air I breathed. I was sure that if I inhaled, the secondhand smoke would land me in a folding chair in a church basement at Narcotics Anonymous. The reason I sat at home and listened to *Born to Run* on my 8-track was that the rock and rollers were not on my team. I did not make it to a Bruce concert until I was forty-two. By then the air was filled with nothing but air.

My parents used to say, "Brett never got in trouble—not once," while I hung my head in shame. What kind of person follows every rule? I was an Amish kid without the *rumspringa*, sure I was missing out.

I am not suggesting that we need more gambling, drinking, and smoking. My sheltered upbringing has advantages. Staying out of trouble is not the worst thing that can happen to you.

The prohibitions with which I grew up seem silly to most teenagers, but this column is not completely out of date. We are still tempted to believe that sin is being on the other team. We divide people into "us" and "them"—Democrats and Republicans, Americans and foreigners, rich and poor. The people outside the church have figured out that sometimes people in the church think of themselves as "us."

What if instead of being taught that sin is playing with the other team, I had been taught that sin is not loving others? How much better would it have been if, rather than feeling superior to the gambling, drinking, and smoking crowd, the church had pointed out that Jesus ran with that crowd? What if we had not been so penny-pinching? What if we had played ball with anyone who wanted to play? What if the church had bought group tickets for Springsteen? What if Christians were known not for prohibitions but for caring?

I am not sure I would have been a better person if I had thrown a penny, taken a drink, or inhaled, but I know I would be farther along if I had not been taught to feel superior to those who did.

What I learned from my eighth-grade teacher in Mississippi in 1975 (July 31, 2018)

Mr. McBrayer threw the barista by ordering "a cup of coffee," which was not on the menu at the Caffeinated Indian. Forty-three years after the eighth grade, I met my social studies teacher at the only coffee shop in Fulton, Mississippi.

In 1975, Mississippi was ranked fiftieth in education and was some distance from being forty-ninth. My school in Saltillo, about thirty miles west of Fulton, reflected our state's poverty, racism, and provincialism. Good teachers like Danny McBrayer fought uphill battles.

During study hall, a group of us were discussing the quickest way to make our first million. Mr. McBrayer told us about driving a school bus, watching the sunrise each morning, and seeing the sunrise change through the year: "I drive the bus for the extra money, but without the sunrise it wouldn't be worth it. Your job needs to be worth it."

In a school that had recently integrated and was painfully divided, Mr. McBrayer went out of his way to spend time with African American students like Ronnie Agnew, now the executive director of Mississippi Public Broadcasting.

Danny McBrayer and his student

Checking in after four decades provides a lot to talk about. Mr. McBrayer knows almost everyone's story. My biology teacher continues to believe that she could have married Elvis. Coach Wright was inducted into the Mississippi Football Hall of Fame. Our principal, who smoked a pipe, died of throat cancer. When I asked about my least favorite teacher, Mr. McBrayer said, "She just never liked poor kids—and that was most of our kids."

My old friends have tragic, predictable, and amazing stories. One of the best athletes in school history is in prison. Two of the three sisters whose names rhymed died years ago, one with cancer and one in a car accident. Bobby got into lots of trouble, became a preacher, and died. Willie has had a hard time: "His family fell apart and he has no legal income."

Jimmy and Dorothy surprised everyone by not getting married. Dorothy ended up with a pro golfer's cousin. Jimmy went through a divorce, but his ex-father-in-law liked him so much that they went into business together. (I'm changing most of these names because I can't read my writing and I'm afraid I may announce a divorce where there is only peace and harmony.)

Lori, on whom most of the eighth grade had a crush, married the quarterback and has done just fine. Joe, the shooting guard on the basketball team, is selling tires. Goony—a nickname I include because he must have left it behind years ago—runs his dad's garage. Peachy (another has-to-have-been-forgotten nickname) is selling satellite dishes.

Craig, the top math student, is an engineer with NASA. Ken, the center on the basketball team, is a high school principal. Todd, who was a great best friend, teaches teachers in Nashville.

Mississippian William Faulkner said, "The past is never done with us. It isn't even past."

So much seems capricious—who lives, who dies, who gets a great job, who gets cancer, whose marriage falls apart, whose child is born with a disability. Telling who's who is hard in middle school, and we do not get much better at it. Even if we could know exactly who someone is, we cannot know how far they have come to get there.

Mississippi makes it clear that the playing field is not level. Some are born with two strikes against them. Some who seem a step behind have made up a mile. Some give themselves to lifelong friendships, honest work, and caring for the hurting.

Those who create lives out of not much make it seem obvious that we should fill our prisons with politicians who lie to poor people while helping rich people keep their advantages. Some who sell tires make more important contributions than some with big corner offices. Some who teach fourteen-year-olds do more good than some preachers.

Paul Ryan and the House chaplain: Proof that prayer works? (April 27, 2018)

Paul Ryan believes in prayer so much that on April 15, 2018, he forced the House chaplain to resign. Ryan has not given a reason for the dismissal, but many are pointing to a prayer Father Patrick Conroy offered while lawmakers were considering tax reform. The priest prayed that lawmakers would "be mindful" of economic disparities and of those "who continue to struggle." Ryan's concern is surprising, as the prayer clearly did not work.

Every once in a while, scientists who cannot raise money for real research get stuck doing a study on how prayer works. Nonbelievers argue that wishful thinking is not a suitable subject for scientific investigation. Believers argue that the results of prayer are not easily measured.

The outcomes of these studies tend to reflect the desires of whoever paid for the research. Religious researchers often find that praying for another's well-being reduces one's own anxiety. Nonreligious researchers point out that prayers for healing are no guarantee that healing will occur.

The scientific study of prayer focuses on the things for which people most often pray—health concerns, financial difficulties, or societal problems—but the prayers we do not pray are the best evidence that prayer works.

Hunger is a subject about which we do not pray. After Jesus told the rich young ruler to sell all that he had and give it to the poor, we can be certain that young man did not go home and pray about it.

We are careful not to pray seriously for the homeless. We find it awkward to pray for people who have no home when we have a guest room.

If we have ever given a gift to a charity, then we do not pray about our mail because most days we get a request for money. Most are worthy causes: the Christian Children's Fund, Habitat for Humanity, Mothers against Drunk Driving, Bread for the World, Alzheimer's research. The message on the envelopes from Amnesty International reads, "You can help stop torture." If we pray over that envelope, we have to write a check.

There are so many situations in which we will not pray. Your boss tells a sexist joke. You know it is evil and wish someone would point it out, but do you really want to pray, "God, what should I do? Should I challenge my boss who might not take kindly to my helpful words of correction?"

We have been praying about gun violence, but we are careful. If you want gun control, it is hard to pray honestly about the sense of moral superiority that may be taking up residence in your heart. If you are a Second Amendment person, it is hard to pray honestly for innocent children who are dying as shooting victims. If we pray seriously about gun violence, we will do more than wait around for the next election.

We do not want to pray about our careers. Does the senior pre-law major want to pray about whether God would like for her to be a social worker? Does the successful businessperson want to ask God if a lower-paying job might make more of a contribution to the world?

We are careful about praying for people we do not like. When Jesus said, "Pray for your enemies," he was inviting us to the kind of prayer that will lead us to say something kind that we do not want to say.

Prayers should come with warnings. Do not pray about the school system; you may end up tutoring second graders. Do not pray about human trafficking; you may end up paying for much-needed supplies for victims. Do not pray about racial justice; you may end up working on bail reform.

We like what we have, especially the vices we have gotten used to. We do not pray about our addictions—eating too much, drinking too much, or spending too much. St. Augustine prayed, "God, give me chastity, but not yet."

Most of us, including Paul Ryan, understand that critiquing prayer is easier than truly praying. We do not avoid praying because our prayers go unanswered. We avoid praying because we are afraid our prayers will be answered. The proof that prayer works is the way we choose a life given to comfort over a life given in prayer.

Flight or invisibility: Revisiting a classic theological question (February 5, 2019)

When I was in middle school, I sat at the philosophers' lunch table. We discussed serious issues: Is a hot dog a sandwich? *The Partridge Family* or *The Brady Bunch*? Wile E. Coyote or the Road Runner? And, more than any other question, flight or invisibility?

We spent hours on this. The rules of the debate were clear. You could not pick both or any alternate powers. If you chose flight, you could fly at the same height and speed as a plane. When you flew, you could carry only what you could already carry in your arms or on your back. You would not get any other superpowers.

Being able to fly would be the key to exciting experiences. We did not, by the way, talk about using our powers for good. We had no illusions about fighting crime. Seeing the world—flying to London for the weekend—would be for the fun of it. If you want to get away, flight sounds great. Choosing flight is choosing freedom.

But I was not sure flight was the right choice. I had questions: How cold is it up high? Are birds a problem? What if you get caught in the rain over the Atlantic? What will you look like on radar? Could you be shot down? I could never quite commit myself to flight. People who choose that kind of freedom may not be happy with where they are now.

The rules for invisibility were also clear. Invisibility is the power to be unseen, including your clothes and anything you might be holding.

Introverts go for invisibility. If you want to be alone, invisibility is great. Invisibility leads to free movies, free plane trips, and shoplifting. You could walk unseen into the White House with a tape recorder and be the world's greatest reporter.

But I had questions about invisibility, too. What happens the first time you get caught? Would being invisible make you creepy? (One student— whom we hope has matured in the last forty-five years—had an unhealthy interest in locker rooms.)

Invisibility leads us to baser instincts, sad places, and bad behavior. Invisibility contributes to the nastiness of the internet. People say things they would not say if they were seen. Invisibility is a superpower for the villain inside us.

Though I never mentioned it at the lunch table because it seemed too personal, every time we debated flight or invisibility, I had the same thought. The superpower I wanted was the ability to stop time.

I had the rules worked out. I could snap my fingers and immobilize everyone and everything except myself. I could stop time for any amount of time. I would do my homework, practice free throws, learn Spanish, play the piano, walk the Appalachian Trail, and write long books, and none of it would take any time. I would read everything by Shakespeare, Hemingway (twice), and Tolkien (three times).

I could stop time for an hour and not have to waste the time it took to mow the lawn. I could hit pause before making a mistake. Stopping time could be helpful if someone wanted to punch me.

I could do so many important things and so many unimportant things. I could stop time to watch *The Six Million Dollar Man*, read every *Archie* comic book, and become an expert at shooting rubber bands. I could stop the clock to think of a clever comeback. I could hibernate for a winter without missing Christmas.

I could waste my time without wasting my time. If I could stop time, I would not leave any box unchecked. I could take the road less traveled, the road more traveled, and some other roads, too.

For decades I thought about stopping time. Now that I'm old (at least by middle school standards), you might think I would be more interested than ever in stopping time. But I have given up on that superpower.

I have come to believe that one of the secrets of life is enjoying the passing of time. Wanting to stop time suggests that I am not happy with the life I have. I have flown to many interesting places (although never Superman-style). And I have felt invisible even though I could still be seen. The superpower I need is the ability to be alive in this moment. I do not want to miss feeling what I have not felt, caring for people I have not cared for, or seeing things that will surprise me.

Paul Tillich talks about the "eternal now"—those moments that touch eternity. I can stop even if the world does not, be quiet in the midst of noise, and slow down enough to notice. I have this moment, and that is enough.

Cultural Commentary

Noah's lawsuit: Is God trying to say something? (May 20, 2019)

The headline reads like a punchline: "Owners of Noah's Ark sue over rain damage." Does God have a sense of humor or what? In the case of *Irony v. This Has to Be a Joke*, Ark Encounter in Williamstown, Kentucky, is suing its insurance carriers.

The administrators of the life-sized replica of Noah's Ark, 300 cubits or 510 feet long, claim that heavy rains, while not reaching biblical proportions, caused a landslide on their access road. The ark itself was not damaged by the flood, nor did the park close, but for a time it looked like people who wanted to get into the ark could not because of the water, just like in the Bible.

The seventy-seven-page lawsuit seeks not only compensatory damages but also punitive damages, presumably because someone made fun of Ark Encounter—which also happened to Noah. The suit asks for a jury trial. They will need to find twelve people with no sense of humor.

Ark Encounter is rumored to have cost $100 million. It opened on July 7, 2016, a date (7/7) that was selected because of Genesis 7:7, "Noah and his sons and his wife and his sons' wives entered the ark to escape the waters of the flood."

They claim to have one million visitors a year. Tickets cost between $15 and $48. Imagine how much money Noah could have made selling tickets.

This story is why Twitter was invented:

"*The Onion* has gone too far."

"Thoughts and prayers!"

"Now I believe in God."

"All right . . . who prayed for rain?"

"I hope the penguins who walked from Antarctica are safe!"

"Looks like God doesn't want anybody to go see it."

"And on the eighth day God created tort reform."

Oh, there's more:

"Seriously, shouldn't Yahweh have prevented this?"

"Noah's replica will have to start an http://godfund.me."

"So biblical . . . just like in Genesis when Noah sued the Lord God for the flood damage to the Earth."

"Mitch McConnell's state. Go figure. Shocker."

"It only carried a 40-day warranty."

"God's will."

If this is a publicity stunt, it is genius. Aren't you tempted to visit? You could be the person who asks too many questions:

Where are the dinosaurs?

How did they fit that many animals in a space that is not big enough for that many animals?

How could there be enough water to cover the whole world?

How did the dogs and cats get along, or the mice and the elephants?

Why didn't the lions eat the bunnies?

Were the bunnies still creating other bunnies?

Were the animals in a coma?

After a month, did Noah wish he was in a coma?

Do you consider the recent rainfall an act of God?

Did you think about suing God and not the insurance company?

How did a story about the annihilation of most of the world's population—men, women, and children drowning, heads bobbing up and down in the water—become an amusement park?

Do you think you might be missing the point?

Noah's ark is not a children's story, a funny story, or even a story concerned with history. This story is true even if it never happened.

If you get past the strangeness, it sounds like recent events. Terrible things are happening to God's good creation. Violence is rampant. Terrorism is on the rise. War is considered a solution. Politicians refuse to listen to their enemies. Children are starving.

We understand their situation. We have had thirteen school shootings this year. We have gotten used to walking past the homeless. Innocent teenagers die in our prisons.

How will God deal with the brokenness of the world? God responds not as an angry architect whose building has been ruined but as a grieving parent whose heart has been broken.

God sees the violence in the world and decides to turn away, forget the whole experience, and walk away. God decides to return creation to the chaos from which God called creation. God will let the waters cover the earth.

But there is one person whom God cannot forget. God's love for Noah changes the plan. The story that, up to now, is all darkness takes a turn to the light.

The grieving God decides to save the world. God will stay with creation, notwithstanding the sorry state of humankind.

After the rain has stopped, God points to the rainbow in the sky and promises never to give up on us. God says, "I take my warrior's bow and restring it not as a weapon, but with the colors of creation."

We travel through waters that threaten to engulf us, but none of the suffering we know comes from God's displeasure. God is doing everything God can do to offer hope, end our heartaches, and bring us home.

That is no joke.

Why Big Bird and Oscar cannot retire (November 12, 2018)

Six-year-olds are going to ask, "Does Big Bird have a cold?" "What's wrong with Oscar?" "Who are they trying to fool?"

Caroll Spinney, the man inside Big Bird and Oscar the Grouch, is retiring after nearly fifty years of delivering comforting lines like "Bad days happen to everyone, but when one happens to you, just keep doing your best" and grouchy lines like "Now leave me alone and get lost!"

Spinney is eighty-four years old and knows what he is doing, but I keep thinking, "What is he doing?"

Where do you go to retire when you have been on Sesame Street since 1969? What neighborhood is going to have such sunny days? Where is the air going to be so sweet? Where will he find such friendly neighbors? Does he understand that there are not many places where everything's A-Okay? How can a retirement community be an improvement when you have lived on a street where birds, monsters, and people coexist in harmony?

Spinney met his wife Debra in 1972 while in the Big Bird costume. What woman would not be impressed? He is going to miss wearing bright yellow feathers and being 8 feet, 2 inches tall.

Big Bird danced with the Rockettes. He has a star on the Hollywood Walk of Fame and his likeness on a stamp. He conducted symphony orchestras. Big Bird starred in his own movie, *Follow That Bird*, and guest starred on *Saturday Night Live*, *The West Wing*, and *The Colbert Report*. He has been the BBF (best bird friend) for so many children. When asked how he could still be six years old after being around for so long, Big Bird replied, "Just lucky, I guess."

Caroll Spinney at the Chiller Theatre Expo, Sheraton Parsippany Hotel in Parsippany, NJ, October 27, 2012.

(Credit: Rob DiCaterino, unaltered photo, https://creativecommons.org/licenses/by/4.0/)

Why would anyone want to leave Sesame Street?

Maybe being inside the Big Bird costume—like Sesame Street itself—is a little claustrophobic. Spinney may feel the need to spread his wings and fly. Perhaps there is a clue in what Big Bird said while in an airplane: "Isn't flying wonderful? It makes me feel like a bird."

On the other hand, do people eventually get tired of sunny days, cloudless skies, and friendly neighbors? Could it be that we can be kind and sweet for only so long?

That is why we need Oscar. What could be more therapeutic than being both Big Bird and Oscar? A tender, nurturing, childlike avian is great, but there is a part of us that is a crabby, trash-talking green monster. Big Bird and Oscar are yin and yang, Jekyll and Hyde, Mary Kate and Ashley. Oscar's different perspective reminds us that there are other perspectives.

Big Bird shows us how to be kind, but Oscar teaches us that it is okay to be grouchy. Sometimes we do not want to talk, and that is fine. We can think—even if we should not say it—"Scram!" "Get lost!" "Go away!" We can be cranky without being a bad person.

Caroll Spinney may that find the world outside his old neighborhood is easier for Oscar than for Big Bird. Most places are not as pristine as Sesame Street. Most air is not that sweet. Some neighbors are more irritating than Bert and Ernie.

Most of us have days when we might as well live in a garbage can. We act like Big Bird while we feel like Oscar. We are gentle, disgruntled, and lovable. We need to be in touch with the grouch that stands up for what is right.

We need the joy of a gargantuan canary, but we also need the feistiness of a complaining Muppet. We need to know that our bad moods are not the end of the world.

That could be how we get to Sesame Street.

Tracking our happiness (May 31, 2018)

Ice queens, awkward teenagers, mediocre wizards, and homeschoolers from Kenya all struggle to be happy. Last week, through a series of fortunate events—a visiting friend, a visiting son, and two *(two!)* wins in the ticket lottery—I ended up attending four Broadway shows in four days. *Frozen; Dear Evan Hansen; Puffs, Or: Seven Increasingly Eventful Years at a Certain School of Magic and Magic;* and *Mean Girls* are about the search for happiness. Our arts, economy, and religion are built on the universal longing for happiness.

We do not smile all the time. What we once found interesting can start to feel like a drag. We fantasize about quitting, moving to Montana, and doing something completely different—like raising ostriches. How hard could it be?

When we see someone moving up, it reminds us that we are not. We liked our job in the beginning, but there are days when we wonder if we have career ADD. The pursuit of happiness is wearing us out.

We are in such a rush that every conversation is a sound bite. Hurrying is admired. Going slow is considered lazy. We are so immersed in the culture of busyness that we do not notice the toll it takes on our health, work, and family.

We think the goal is to get what we want, and there is always more to want. What kind of economy would we have if we believed that not getting what we want could make us as happy as getting what we want?

In his TED Talk on happiness, research psychologist Dan Gilbert claims that a year after winning the lottery and a year after losing the use of their legs, lottery winners and those confined to wheelchairs are equally happy. We assume happiness is the result of circumstances, but the research does not support that. Studies suggest that passing a test, losing a romantic partner, and getting a promotion have less impact, intensity, and duration than we expect.

What we have learned about happiness sounds too simple. Trackyour-happiness is a phone app that works like an iPhone therapist. At random moments, your phone pings and asks what you are experiencing in that moment. How do you feel right now? Do you have to do what you are doing? To what extent are you being productive? Do you want to do what you are doing? Are you thinking about something other than what you are doing?

More than 35,000 people have made more than a half-million responses. The most consistent finding is that when we are trying to go in more than one direction, we are less happy. When the thirty-second peek at Twitter becomes ten minutes, we become less happy. When we are not focused on things that matter, we complain. Forty-seven percent of the time, we are thinking of something other than what we are doing.

Happiness is more in our heads than in our circumstances. We know people who have what we want who are unhappy. We know people who have been through the worst that life can give who are happy.

In 1962, the manager of a Liverpool rock band fired the group's twenty-year-old drummer. Pete Best had been playing with the band for two years. Just weeks after Best was kicked out, "Love Me Do" began to climb the charts. Pete Best cried. He worked for a while in a bakery. Then he put together his own group—the Pete Best Band. He toured the world with his brother and three other band members.

Best, seventy-six, and his wife, Kathy, have now been married for forty-nine years. They have two daughters and four grandchildren, whom Best says he "totally spoils." He describes himself as a family man who is always happy to come home to Liverpool: "I believe it turned out for the best. I enjoy every day twice as much as the day before. I'm happier than I would have been with the Beatles."

Maybe he is telling the truth. Shakespeare argues, "Tis nothing good or bad but thinking makes it so." Not quite. A trip to Paris is better than a colonoscopy, but we have more control over our happiness than we admit.

No matter what problem brings them to him, psychologist Shawn Achor has his new patients write down three new things for which they are grateful every day for twenty-one days. The research suggests that this practice inclines our brains to scan the world for the positive.

Queens, teenagers, wizards, and homeschoolers are just a few of the groups that need a more thoughtful perspective. We all need to ask how much better our lives would be if we believed what is clearly true. The happiness that comes when we are grateful is more real than what comes when we get what we thought we wanted.

People I don't need to listen to (April 13, 2017)

The *New York Times* has too many pages. I download more podcasts than I can play. I cannot read half of what my friends post on *Facebook*—particularly one recipe-happy friend. I cannot hear, read, or notice a significant portion of what is calling for my attention.

People who claim to know such things say that listeners can follow 1.2 conversations at a time. I can completely follow one conversation and one-fifth of another. I can catch half of two conversations and one-fifth of the third. I can follow three-fifths of two conversations. But I cannot hear it all.

Some news shows feature three conversations going at the same time. The assumption seems to be that we will listen to whoever shouts the loudest. I cannot hear over the cacophony, so I have concluded that I need to listen less.

I need to ignore some conversations. I do not need to hear people who do not listen themselves, who do not empathize, or whose voices are full of hatred.

I should be leery of people who are paid to offer opinions. People who use their judgments to get wealthier are not the first people I need to hear.

I can stop reading editorials that only repeat what I already think. I can give a rest to my habit of flipping through channels to find someone saying what I want to hear.

I should not listen to people whose job is to defend bad ideas. I can turn off commentators who tell prejudiced people that they are not prejudiced.

I do not need to hear people who come to conclusions too easily. Listening to those who do not care is not the best use of my time.

I do not need to hear white people explaining what it is like to be black. I should listen to the victims of prejudice.

I do not need to hear those who critique Islam without having read the Koran. I should listen to committed Muslims.

I do not need to hear mean-spirited people with no evidence who enjoy saying that immigrants are the reason their cousin cannot find a job. I should listen to hard-working immigrants and the children of immigrants.

As the Department of Education abandons the poor, I do not need to hear those who have never been inside a public school discuss education. I need to listen to teachers.

I do not need to hear politicians who are on the payroll of gun manufacturers talk about the right to own an AK-47. I should listen to grieving parents.

I do not need to hear wealthy people pontificate on health care. I should listen to the sick, the elderly, and doctors in underserved areas.

I do not need to hear someone in a thousand-dollar suit telling poor people how to manage their finances. I should listen to the ones who struggle to put food on the table.

I do not need to hear those who do not care about children escaping from Syria, bigoted people who do not have gay friends, or rich men on their third marriage who want to tell a poor woman what to do about her pregnancy. I should listen more to refugees, committed gay couples, and those with a uterus.

I need to hear people who do not sound like me. I need to listen to those who do not have a Twitter account. If the person I am listening to does not really love, then I am giving myself permission not to listen. I cannot hear everyone, so I need to listen more to those who are not often heard.

My undelivered stand-up routine for those not likely to come back to church (April 5, 2018)

How is everybody doing tonight? You look great. You're less sober than the people I usually talk to.

I'm surprised to be at the Comedy Cellar because—and I know how this sounds—I'm a minister. Saying that you're a minister shuts down conversations with barbers, waitresses, and the person sitting next to you on the plane. That last one is helpful.

I'm not a minister who thinks he's cool enough to fit in anywhere. I'm not the Unitarian campus minister at NYU. I don't wear a tweed jacket and a turtleneck. I don't run a soup kitchen in Hell's Kitchen. I don't actually do the stuff I tell everyone else to do. I'm not the chaplain for U2—which is not a real job—but I can dream.

My church isn't Episcopal, so I don't get paid much. My church isn't a rock-and-roll church, so I don't wear jeans to work. My church isn't a Pentecostal church, so I'm not on any medication.

Think of it this way. Episcopal churches are the New York Philharmonic. Rock-and-roll churches are Coldplay. Pentecostals are the Sex Pistols. I'm the minister at a Congregational church, which is Adele—and who doesn't like Adele?

You might be surprised to learn that churches talk about some of you a lot.

How many of you went to church more often when you were nine years old?

You're the ones churches talk about. Churches think they can get you back. Churches are your mother trying to get you to come home for the weekend by promising the beef noodle casserole she insists you loved when you were a kid.

Like your parents, churches think you don't come home because you're embarrassed by them. We understand. Most churches are embarrassed by other churches.

Lots of people who go to church voted for Trump, which leaves churches like mine wanting to put up big signs that say, "We're not like them. We swear. Damn it."

Some churches think they'll get you to come back with bad drummers. They believe there are twenty-year-olds who wake up early on Sunday mornings and say to themselves, "I feel like singing along with a sixty-year-old drummer playing eighteenth-century hymns."

Some churches have started meeting in pubs for "Theology on Tap," where they drink beer and talk about God. They hope you're looking for an inebriated minister to explain the meaning of life.

Some churches have changed their names with you in mind. If a church has a name that sounds like a '70s band—Journey, Passion, The Bridge, Scum of the Earth—you're the target audience.

Some churches still have people who literally believe in some crazy stuff—talking bushes, talking snakes, and talking donkeys—but we also have people who think just about everything is a metaphor for things you like—peace, love, and joy.

We know the church can be disappointing, but we also know the church can be wonderful. If you decide to give us another chance, we'll try not to act cooler than we are. We'll learn your name and ask how you're doing. We'll find gracious ways to say that we find hope in believing in something bigger than we are, and we think you might, too. You can help us with hard questions about meaning and purpose. You can help us do things rather than just talk about them. You might find that you enjoy being part of a group of friends trying to live more authentically.

Deep down, we know that you're probably not coming back, but we hope it's comforting for you to know that someone is thinking of you.

When the Klan came to our revival (July 10, 2015)

Melanie was—depending on who you talked to—sharing the love of Christ or trying to cause trouble. Forty-five years later, I like to think it was both. Nixon was president, gas was 36 cents a gallon, and everything in my hometown was separate and unequal.

My father was the pastor of Calvary Baptist Church in West Point, Mississippi. The people at Calvary encouraged me to fear anyone who did not look like us. We understood that there are Bible verses about God's love for all people, but we ignored them. We sang "red and yellow, black and white" without realizing how offensive it was. The sign out front said, "Everyone is welcome." We knew how to read the sign.

For our youth revival in the church gym, we invited an evangelist who knew how to get middle schoolers to walk the aisle. The preacher would explain to the ones who had not been baptized that they could be hit by a bus on the way home and burn in hell forever. The ones who had strayed into sin must promise never to commit that sin again—not even if she is a cheerleader. The ones who had not strayed into sin because no cheerleader would ever invite them to do so needed to give in to God's call to ministry. Anyone who was not 100 percent certain of their eternal resting place should walk the aisle because what could it hurt? We lined up Miss Mississippi and a quarterback from Mississippi State to speak because this was big-time worship.

Melanie, a seventh grader, invited her best friend Carlene, an African American, to witness the glory of our youth revival. Melanie and Carlene made their way to folding chairs near midcourt. The ushers gathered to decide how to deal with this thirteen-year-old threat to their Christianity. Wayne, a Little League baseball coach, asked Carlene to leave. Melanie went with her.

The next night, two members of the Klan and the deacon board were stationed at the gym door to make sure no African Americans tried to worship God. They did not wear the hoods—which would have been more honest. Nothing interesting happened.

Years later it finally occurred to me to ask, "How unimpressed would Carlene have been if she had stayed?"

Our church sang Fanny Crosby hymns. We reassured ourselves with "Blessed assurance, Jesus is mine," comforted ourselves with the promise that "He hideth our souls in the cleft of the rock," and encouraged ourselves with the certainty that we were "Redeemed" and "loved to proclaim it." But the African American churches across town got to sing "Swing Low,

Sweet Chariot," "I Want Jesus to Walk with Me," and "His Eye Is on the Sparrow." Their songs were better.

They had Aretha Franklin. We had the Bill Gaither Trio. Their singers were better.

They had Martin Luther King Jr. We had Jerry Falwell. They were proclaiming "a dream that one day even the state of Mississippi, a state sweltering with the heat of injustice, will be transformed into an oasis of freedom and justice." We were trying to preserve an oasis of injustice. Their preachers were better.

The people at Carlene's church sang, prayed, and worshiped more honestly than we did at Calvary. How disappointed would Carlene have been if she had gotten to stay?

I thought about this last Sunday while worshiping at Antioch AME Church in Stone Mountain, Georgia. Carol and I have been to Antioch six times because I need to learn to experience rather than critique worship.

We go to sing. I try to sing, clap, and sway at the same time. The soloists make me want to feel what they feel.

We go to give. The pastor is willing to tell us exactly how much. Last Sunday we gave three offerings.

We go to pray. Sometimes the prayers go where I am not used to hearing them go. Prayers that start with gratitude for a job may end up imploring God to get other people a job "right now."

I go and wonder what would have happened if Melanie had gone to church with Carlene. Would Melanie have ever come back to Calvary? What I could not see when I was nine years old is clear: God wanted us to join Carlene's revival.

Bracketology theology: Who would Jesus pick? (March 18, 2014)

NCAA college basketball tournament brackets are being emailed, faxed, and taped on refrigerators. Many fans will make their picks without reflecting on the theological implications.

Unfortunately, some with no real love for basketball are filling out brackets. People who do not care will pick Virginia because of Aunt Virginia, Wisconsin-Milwaukee because of *Laverne and Shirley*, San Diego State because of Ron Burgundy, Colorado because of John Denver, Dayton because of the Wright Brothers, Stanford because of Condoleezza Rice, Kentucky because of Ashley Judd, and George Washington because of George Washington.

They will pick Brigham Young to take out Oregon because a duck would not have a chance against a cougar. Picking between the Arizona Wildcats and Weber State Wildcats, as well as the Kentucky Wildcats and the Kansas State Wildcats, is confusing. The Villanova Wildcats are taking on the Wisconsin-Milwaukee Panthers, which is hard to pick. Thankfully, those Panthers are not likely to meet the Pitt Panthers.

Most nicknames show little imagination, so it is hard not to love the Albany Great Danes, Coastal Carolina Chanticleers, Delaware Blue Hens, Louisiana-Lafayette Ragin' Cajuns, Manhattan Jaspers, Massachusetts Beacons, Saint Louis Billikens, Stephen F. Austin Lumberjacks, and Xavier Musketeers.

Many will not care if their picks actually win, but if some tiny team like the Wofford Terriers beats some big dog like the Michigan Wolverines, these prognosticators will think they are Jimmy the Greek. We know deep down that it is wrong to pick against Kentucky because their players don't go to class or to pick for Cal Poly because it sounds like a dental product.

Basketball matters. Indifference runs contrary to the Christian faith. Jesus cares; so should his followers.

Others have learned that picking Texas Southern to win it all will leave you without a team two hours into the tournament, so they throw in with the experts. Favoring the favorites is the easy way. They cast their lots with No. 1 seeds—Florida, Wichita State, Arizona, and Virginia. They bet that 2s will always beat 15s, 3s over 14s, and 8s over 9s. They give up on high hoops hopes and give themselves only to the solid hardwood of the expected. If there are no upsets, they will have their bracket laminated. These people are no fun to play with.

Something is desperately wrong with doing what is safe. God does not call us to be sensible. People of faith do not carefully weigh the alternatives. Jesus lived beyond prudence; so should his followers.

People of faith eschew apathy and predictability. We belong to a different world from the one where big schools with big players and big money win all the big games. We follow our hoop dreams.

We give our hearts to directional schools (North Carolina Central, Western Michigan), states that do not sound like states (San Diego State, Weber State) and schools that are not often on national television (Albany, Coastal Carolina).

We take seriously the religious inferences of our choices. Because we like the new pope, we look favorably at the Catholic schools (Creighton, Dayton, Gonzaga, Manhattan, Providence, Saint Joseph's, Saint Louis, Villanova, and Xavier). Because we like not having a pope and do not have nine schools in the big dance, we are sympathetic toward the Baptist schools (Baylor and Mercer).

The first round features a clash between two universities that have divinity schools—Duke and Mercer—but Duke is the Blue Devils, which sounds like they are cheering for the other team, so serious theologians cheer for the Bears. Our love for the Mercers in this tournament may keep us from winning the office pool, but Jesus calls us to hope.

What is the point of living in the world of boring brackets when we can live in the vibrant rainbow that dreams are made of? Why wouldn't we choose a world in which a Baptist school with little athletic tradition and not enough rebounding could take the trophy?

Picking with our hearts may be madness, but the faith-filled choose the NCAA tournament of what should be. People of faith believe that David will defeat Goliath. We do not give ourselves to what is most likely. We dream of a tournament and a world that is better than it is.

Why I had an Egg McMuffin this morning (August 1, 2012)

I boycotted Chick-fil-A for years. This is not an excuse, but I grew up in Southern Baptist churches in the Deep South. I am embarrassed as I look back on my narrow-mindedness, but this is what I truly believed:

Cows who write "Eat Mor Chikin" on poster board are not natural. The cows in my hometown did not make posters. If any of our cows did make posters, then they kept their alternative spellings secret.

Misspelling words like "mor" and "chikin" will make others misspell words. Poor spelling is as catching as chikin pox.

Encouraging misspelling cows will open the door to other kinds of immoral behavior. People will want misspelling cats and dogs. Soon no one will remember how to spell "correctly," or "chicken" for that matter.

Cows who spell correctly feel threatened by misspelling cows. To make traditional cows feel comfortable, we need to be clear on what the one correct spelling of each word is.

If we treat cows like other spelling beings, we will "eat mor chikin," and that's their agenda.

Normal cows are acceptable because they produce normal calves. Can we trust Chick-fil-A cows as parents?

Jesus never said anything about cows with poor spelling. We can only assume he hated them.

So for years I kept my distance. I stayed in my little bubble. I thought if I ignored them, they would go away. When Chick-fil-A commercials came on television, I hit mute. When their ads were on the radio, I changed to a station that agreed with me on this issue. When I passed Chick-fil-A billboards, I turned my head. I not only felt superior to the people at Chick-fil-A; I felt superior to the people who defended them.

I had nothing to do with Chick-fil-A chicken sandwiches for years. This was what I was taught. This was what I believed. Questioning these orthodox views would be wrong.

Then one day my most open-minded friend pulled into a Chick-fil-A. I expected to hear myself say, "We're going to McDonald's like real Americans," but I didn't. I'm not sure why. I felt like some spirit was pulling me beyond my bigotry. My provincial world was about to be rocked.

When we went inside, I started sweating like Angus at a steakhouse. I wasn't sure how or what to order. I didn't grow up with chicken Caesar cool wraps or chargrilled chicken garden salads. Doesn't "spicy chicken sandwich deluxe" seem a bit much? Why don't they serve hamburgers like everyone else?

But after my initial discomfort, I realized that it was not what I expected. The young men at the counter were not threatening but were friendly and helpful. The menu was spelled correctly and punctuated properly. No one tried to talk me into ordering what they liked. I bought a chicken biscuit and a cup of coffee. They tasted like my mother made them. I began to wonder if having chicken as well as hamburger places was okay. My old prejudices didn't make sense. Why was I taught that different is wrong?

Since then I have often picked up a chicken biscuit and a decaf coffee at Chick-fil-A on the way to work.

Today was Chick-fil-A Appreciation Day. Customers lined up to support the CEO's support of homophobia. I went to McDonald's.

True Beliebers (February 18, 2014)

When Justin Bieber was arrested in January for drinking, driving, and drag racing, it was front-page news and a goldmine for late-night comics.

Jay Leno opened with an announcement from President Obama: "America's number one domestic terrorist was arrested today . . . . We don't have to live in fear anymore." Jimmy Fallon thought Jaybee's rented Lamborghini was "surprising when you hear that the only race car he had been in before that was his bed." David Letterman's "Top 10 Justin Bieber Headlines We're Likely to Read" included "Jury enters third day of belieberations," "Bieber, Kardashian married," and "Bieber, Kardashian finalize divorce." Jimmy Kimmel went with, "Just when the streets are finally safe from Lindsay Lohan, Justin Bieber comes out of nowhere."

According to the *New York Post*, on February 1 Bieber looked for a private pool to conduct a baptism but could not find an appropriate place. Bieber has attended worship at Hillsong Church in Manhattan. After a service in September, he tweeted about Pastor Carl Lentz: "Amazing sermon at church this morning. Love you man. I broke down today."

One source said, "Justin is serious about his Christian faith, and after recent events, he needed to take a pause." My eighteen-year-old niece Paityn—who once labeled this "The Bieber Decade"—points out that the young Canadian sings a song titled "Pray."

We should not be surprised that the media has not made a big deal of the Teenage Dream's attempted baptism, but you might guess the church would have a different reaction. In response to the news that the world's most famous teenager wanted to be baptized, Christian leaders have said . . . well, have you heard anything? Are any churches having conversations about how wonderful it is that God is at work in Justin's life?

The church's reluctance to celebrate the Biebs' decision is understandable. J-Beebs does not seem like the kid you ask to preach on Youth Sunday. Raids of his tour buses have turned up a stun gun, narcotics, and marijuana. He allegedly slugged a limo driver and egged his neighbors' house. (Leave it to Bieber.) "Baby" and "One Less Lonely Girl" are not Sunday morning songs.

Laughing at Bieberlicious along with everybody else is easy, but how cynical do we want to be? Shouldn't the church set aside our suspicion and consider the possibility that this is not a publicity stunt? Could JB be genuinely reflecting on what faith in Christ means? We are supposed to be the ones who believe in baptism, repentance, and God giving drag-racing pop singers second chances. If Justin had called St. Peter from the Miami Beach police station and asked what to do next, wouldn't the Apostle say, "Repent and be baptized"?

Do we believe that God turns around egg-throwing nineteen-year-olds? Can we imagine that God helps rich kids who drive under the influence? Should Biebtacular be on our prayer lists? Has anyone offered the Biebernator the use of their baptistery? Has any church put a sign out front that says, "Come on in, JBiebs, the water's fine"?

Beibs Baby could do the church a lot of good, but that is not the point. God means for the church to be a refuge to which anyone can go for comfort—drinkers, smokers, musicians, and drag racers. Christianity has a lot to say about righteousness, but morality is not the theme. The primary hope of the Christian faith is *not* that we will stop egging houses or driving too fast but that we will recognize how God loves us all in spite of our foolish ways. Maybe we should set aside our skepticism and belieb it.

Replacing Sarah Palin (January 31, 2011)

Remember how sad you felt when WJM-TV was sold and Mary Tyler Moore had to find a new job, Hawkeye came home from Korea, or *The Sopranos* faded to black? Many are feeling the same kind of loss now that their favorite TV family is done.

The devastating news is that there are no plans to produce more episodes of *Sarah Palin's Alaska*, despite Palin's blockbuster ratings—an average of 3.2 million viewers.

No one is caught in the crosshairs. This is no blood-libel vendetta on anyone's part. *Entertainment Weekly*—a primary source for in-depth analysis—reported that if Sarah appeared in more shows and then ran for office, The Learning Channel would have to provide other candidates equal time. Apparently, TLC does not want to air *Mike Huckabee's Arkansas*, *Mitt Romney's Massachusetts*, or *Tim Pawlenty's Minnesota*.

No matter how fine the other Republicans' reality shows might have been—imagine the possibilities of *Haley Barbour's Mississippi*—they would have a difficult time recreating the thrills of Sarah's show.

The former governor and her family shared the wonders of the state they love. They fished for salmon, hiked glaciers, rafted white waters, panned for gold, climbed rocks, tracked caribou, and cooked halibut. Along the way they encountered fascinating characters and lots of bears. For eight episodes, Sarah led viewers to glory in the splendors of the great Alaskan wilderness.

Nature abhors a vacuum, and Sarah left an empty space as big as the country's largest state. The Learning Channel has to be looking desperately, so here is a great idea for their next great reality show—*Brett Younger's Church*.

Follow me as I lead viewers into the glorious wilderness of church ministry. The former pastor and his family (my children are every bit as photogenic as Bristol and Piper) will share the wonders of churches we love.

Brett will explore churches fishing for new members, hike the halls during Sunday school while hunting for Krispy Kremes, raft the treacherous waters of a deacons' meeting, pan for gold during a stewardship campaign, climb the rocks of church conflict, track wandering youth at a lock-in, and cook fish for Wednesday night supper. Along the way viewers will encounter fascinating characters and a few bears.

Picture the first episode, "The Pastor's Week." The pastor counsels a couple who shouldn't get married but has already bought the dress, explains to the finance committee that the preschool rooms can't go another year without new Lincoln logs, enlightens the Lord's Supper committee as to why they can go another year without gold-plated serving trays, writes an article about how the church is staying current so that he can later beg a twenty-year-old to put it on the website, negotiates with the administrator for medium-quality beige copy paper for the order of worship, and tactfully suggests that the youth minister limit the number of "likes" and "justs" in the prayer of confession.

The audience will follow the preacher into the study and thrill to exegeting the text, parsing the Greek, studying the historical setting, checking commentaries, outlining the sermon, struggling for the perfect key idea, and resisting the temptation to click on desperatepreacher.com.

Viewers will delight to watch the minister debrief Sunday's service with a self-appointed worship consultant, respond to a short email from someone who thinks the pastor is "God's gift to our church," and reply to a long email from someone who thinks the church is "going rogue."

Eight episodes will not be nearly enough to explore the amazing characters who populate this final frontier: Annie Mae, who has been teaching Bible verses to third graders for thirty years; Emily, who comes every Sunday morning even though her mother is still sleeping off Saturday night; Jim, who takes thirty minutes to maneuver his walker from his car to his pew. The audience will be enchanted by these real saints who keep coming to church to give themselves to God.

Since Sarah is not using it any more, her old show's song, "Follow Me There," will make a fine theme for *Brett Younger's Church*:

> You need a place to be your sanctuary,
> come on, follow me there.
> Where love like a river flows,
> peace like you've never known,
> joy never ending is.
> A place where faith can find
> hope that will never die.

Tell the truth. Doesn't that sound more like the church than a bear-infested wilderness?

The many things I do not know about racism (January 16, 2017)

Two years ago, Carol and I started attending a nearby African Methodist Episcopal Church. One other white person came from time to time. I liked it more when she was not there because I enjoyed saying, "We were the only white people at church."

One Sunday, the pastor surprised me by calling me to the platform to lead the morning prayer. Everything I said brought a response. I am not sure if "Help him, Holy Ghost" is encouragement or critique.

On June 17, 2015, Dylann Roof went to a prayer meeting at the Emanuel AME Church in Charleston, South Carolina, and murdered nine people. People like me thought it was an isolated incident, but my African American friends knew better. Dylann Roof had been taught to hate. He breathed the air of racism.

Two days later I got a call from the pastor of the church we were attending: "The minister who was killed is a member of my family. I'm going to Charleston. Could you preach this Sunday?"

What I said was, "I'm so sorry, but I'm in Texas right now for a conference. I've agreed to preach at a church here on Sunday. I'm very sorry."

But what I thought was, "What would I say? What could I possibly say? What could a white preacher say to broken-hearted African Americans who have fears I can't even imagine?"

I have an easier life because of the color of my skin. I have privileges I do not recognize. I breathe the air of racism. I was taught to have a sense of superiority and to consider condescension charity. When I reach into my wallet, ignore the twenties, and get a dollar bill to drop into a poor person's hand, I do not think about the part privilege and prejudice played in that person's homelessness.

Last week as we felt the anguish of victims' families at Dylann Roof's sentencing, I wondered what I would say if I had another chance to preach at the AME church. At least this:

I want to understand what you deal with, but I also know that it might break my heart.

I do not know what it is like to have nightmares of a church service that ends in murder.

I do not know what it is like be the mother of a teenage son who is afraid because her son's skin is the same color as the skin of Trayvon Martin, Michael Brown, Eric Garner, Jamar Clark, and Tamir Rice.

I do not know what it is like to be an African American in a country where the president has a history of racist comments that includes insulting heroes of the civil rights movement.

I do not know what it is like to be an African American and know that the attorney general once suggested that a white civil rights attorney was a traitor to his race for taking a voting rights case.

I do not know what it is like to be complimented on how articulate you are and wonder if that is a compliment only black people receive.

I do not know what it is like to drive knowing you are more likely to be pulled over by the police.

I do not know what it is like to be looked at with suspicion by store clerks because of the color of your skin.

I do not know what it is like to know that some people who have never met you do not want you living next door.

I do not know what it is like to fear that your child's teacher expects less of your child.

I do not know what it is like to realize that some of the churches that sing "in Christ there is no east or west" would not welcome you.

I do not know what it is like to truly hear the shameful silence of white Christians.

Paying Attention to Politics

Ministers telling people how to vote (November 1, 2018)

Ministers who are sane do not want to tell people how to vote.

If the minister is in the majority of a red or blue congregation, then taking a side is picking on the one guy who wears a MAGA hat to the potluck or the one woman who has an *I'm too poor to vote Republican* bumper sticker on her Prius. If the minister is in the minority, then he or she can survive only a limited number of endorsements. If the congregation is evenly divided between Democrats and Republicans, then championing candidates is asking for angry emails.

Being a minister has gotten harder since the 2016 election. When a sermon refers to President Trump by name, the preacher has to answer for it during coffee hour. Mentioning poverty, integrity, or compassion sounds political. Speaking against greed, violence, xenophobia, homophobia, or sexism is controversial.

Politics is depressing because some important religious issues are not listed in either party's talking points.

Caring for the poor is a religious issue. The world's great faiths insist on feeding the hungry. While officials argue over who represents the middle class, only a few put forth policies that offer poor families a real chance.

War is a religious issue. Many seem to have forgotten that our nation has troops in Afghanistan. The suggestion that we love our enemies would sound strange on who-can-scream-the-loudest talk shows.

Telling the truth is a religious issue. Politicians have a shrinking concern for accuracy. Constituents give their side a free pass.

Few politicians make serious efforts to consider how free trade could alleviate hunger, basic medical coverage could ease suffering, or concern for justice in the international arena could reduce anger towards our country.

Religious people are smart enough to consider issues beyond the last partisan punchline. Immigration, prison reform, and the environment matter to religious people because faith has something to say about hospitality, revenge, and creation.

Imagine how good government could be if those who say God is love took love for the poor, the desire for peace, and an insistence on honesty into the voting booth. What wonderful things would happen if our values were derived from virtue rather than partisanship?

Sincere people of faith vote for different candidates for reasons deeply rooted in their faith. They disagree on how to educate children, promote racial understanding, and support gender equality, but they share frustration with politicians who appeal to individual interests, national interests, and special interests. Religious faith leads away from narrow-mindedness to concern for the good of others.

Religious organizations have no business endorsing candidates, but they have an obligation to share the best of their traditions.

Ministers do not get to avoid the call for justice in order to avoid appearing political.

Religious people disagree on how to care for refugees, but ministers have to preach that it is not acceptable to separate children from their parents.

Religious people disagree on what a prison should look like, but ministers have to preach care for those who are imprisoned.

Religious people disagree on how to respond to victims of sexual assault, but ministers have to preach the necessity of listening.

Religious people can offer ideas beyond politics as usual, speaking for political reform where the insights of faith intersect societal concerns. The movements for civil rights, women's suffrage, and child labor laws began with religious people. When debates focus on which candidate will make voters richest, religious people can be a voice for the oppressed.

The United States is a remarkable country with lofty goals. Even when disappointed by the choices, religious people appreciate the privilege of voting. Ministers should encourage their congregations to pay attention to more than the superficial and vote with concern for all.

President Trump, you could make things easier for preachers (February 16, 2017)

Dear President Trump:

I am sure you are getting letters from groups that feel like they are being mistreated. Muslims, Hispanics, African Americans, women, Jews, the poor, and the LGBTQ community have legitimate concerns, but have you thought about how you are making life difficult for preachers? Ministers are not usually considered an oppressed group, but preaching was easier before you became president.

Most preachers are not looking for trouble. We do not want to offend church members. We have little interest in partisan politics. We try to be respectful of those who do not vote as we do. Preachers say things like, "We are not all going to agree," "Good people have different opinions," and "My mother never votes like I do and she's a fine person."

But you are making it hard. On the Sunday before Martin Luther King Jr. Day, I was preaching on racism. I finished preparing the sermon on Friday afternoon. On Saturday you sent a tweet insulting John Lewis: "All talk, talk, talk—no action or results. Sad!" How could I preach on bigotry on Martin Luther King Jr. weekend and not mention the president picking a fight with a civil rights hero? If you feel like you have to do things like this, it would be helpful if you would do them early in the week so preachers do not have to rewrite their sermons on Saturday night.

You may not even recognize that you keep doing this. The first lectionary reading for January 29 was Micah 6:8: "What does God require of you, but that you do justice, love kindness, and walk humbly with your God?" On Friday afternoon, you enacted an executive order that suspended entry of refugees from seven predominantly Muslim countries. How could preachers ignore you coming out against justice, kindness, and humility toward these people?

The first reading for February 5 was Isaiah 58:6-7: "Is not this the fast I choose: to loose the bonds of injustice, to undo the thongs of the yoke, to let the oppressed go free?" On Saturday morning, you tweeted about a federal judge: "The opinion of this so-called judge, which essentially takes law-enforcement away from our country, is ridiculous and will be overturned!" How could a minister preach on the oppressed going free without mentioning that the president is trying to force the oppressed back into bondage?

The Gospel reading for February 12, Matthew 5:21-37, was Jesus saying, "If you insult a brother or sister, you will be liable to the council, and if you say, 'You fool,' you will be liable to the hell of fire." Lots of ministers spent February 11 worrying that you would call someone a fool. You have, according to *The Mirror*, insulted more than 100 brothers and sisters on Twitter including Meryl Streep, Jeb Bush, Ronda Rousey, Arnold Schwarzenegger, Samuel L. Jackson, Megyn Kelly, Nordstrom's, Mexico and the musical *Hamilton.*

How can ministers preach on telling the truth without using the phrase "alternative facts"? How can we preach on equality without noting that you have said horrible things about women? How can we preach on caring for the hurting without pointing out that you plan to cancel health insurance for 20 million people? How can we preach on the biblical command to welcome strangers without commenting on the wall you want to build to keep them out?

Preachers do not have a choice. We have to preach that God loves all people and does not believe in America first. If we preach the Gospel, some are going to think we are taking shots at you. You are forcing preachers either to mention you or to look hopelessly out of touch. If we do not respond to the things you say, then some will assume we are asleep at the pulpit. Do we risk offending church members or feeling like cowards?

You could make our lives easier. You could replace the Affordable Care Act with the More Affordable Care Act. You could work to alleviate hunger. You could strengthen our commitment to education. You could diminish the spread of terrorism by lessening the causes of terrorism. You could make the lives of so many people better. Some of them are preachers.

The Gospel text for this coming Sunday, Matthew 5:38-48, is, "You have heard that it was said, 'An eye for an eye and a tooth for a tooth.' . . . But I say to you, Love your enemies and pray for those who persecute you." Please do not give us anything to preach about.

Sincerely,
Rev. Brett Younger
Plymouth Church, Brooklyn, New York

Why aren't more Christians refusing service? (October 2, 2015)

Kim Davis's fifteen minutes of fame have stretched to fifteen weeks. Just after the Supreme Court affirmed the right of same-sex couples to marry, Davis affirmed the right of county clerks to decide who can get married. She refused to serve gay couples seeking marriage licenses, and then when that turned out to be illegal, she refused to serve any couples who wanted to get married. Davis was making a federal judge crazy, so he threw her in jail.

When that move put the jail on the list of tourist attractions in Kentucky and the judge on the list of people Kim Davis's fans harass, the judge let Kim inspire people from home. She met with the pope to explain what real religious persecution looks like. Kim has taken the law into her own hands in order to encourage Christians to refuse service to others.

Some have suggested that if Davis does not want to do her job, she should consider other employment, but why should she have to change jobs just because she does not want to do the job she agreed to do? Perhaps her refusal to serve those she promised to serve is unreasonable, but where has being reasonable ever gotten us?

More Christians should refrain from providing services. Every Christian has a responsibility to follow biblical laws even when it makes no sense. More Christians could be on the front page if they took the rules as seriously as Kim does. Here are stories for which we should not have to wait:

Kim Davis herself could get us started by refusing to recognize her own marriage license because Kim has been married four times: "Wherefore they are no more twain, but one flesh. What therefore God hath joined together, let not man put asunder" (Matt 19:6).

Christian bakers—some of whom already refuse to make cakes for gay couples—should refuse to make cakes for fat people: "The glutton shall come to poverty" (Prov 23:21).

Christian ministers should refuse to say the prayer *before* a meal: "When thou hast eaten and art full, then thou shalt bless the LORD thy God" (Deut 8:10).

Christian doctors should refuse to treat sick preachers: "Six days shall work be done, but on the seventh day there shall be to you a holy day, a Sabbath of rest to the LORD: whosoever doeth work therein shall be put to death" (Exod 35:2).

Christian dermatologists should refuse to treat anyone with a tattoo: "Ye shall not make any cuttings in your flesh for the dead, nor print any marks upon you" (Lev 19:28).

Christian grocers should refuse to buy produce from farmers who raise two crops in the same field: "Thou shalt not sow thy field with mingled seed" (Lev 19:19).

Christian cooks should refuse to make shrimp scampi: "And all that have not fins and scales in the seas, and in the rivers, of all that move in the waters, and of any living thing which is in the waters, they shall be an abomination unto you" (Lev 11:10).

Christian hair dressers should refuse to braid hair: "Women adorn themselves in modest apparel, with shamefacedness and sobriety; not with braided hair" (1 Tim 2:9).

Christian jewelers should refuse to sell anything "gold, or pearls, or costly array" (1 Tim 2:9).

Christian men should refuse to marry normal women: "But I suffer not a woman to teach, nor to usurp authority over the man, but to be in silence" (1 Tim 2:12).

Christian bus drivers should refuse to drive to events that offend their sensibilities—WrestleMania, Taylor Swift concerts, Joel Osteen crusades: "Abstain from all appearance of evil" (1 Thess 5:22).

Christian politicians should refuse to participate in the pledge of allegiance: "Swear not at all; neither by heaven; for it is God's throne. Nor by the earth; for it is his footstool. Neither by Jerusalem; for it is the city of the great King" (Matt 5:34-35).

Christian cashiers should refuse to sell guns: "They shall beat their swords into plowshares, and their spears into pruning hooks" (Isa 2:4).

Christian citizens should refuse to pay taxes because the money goes to pay for weapons: "Blessed are the peacemakers: for they shall be called the children of God" (Matt 5:9).

Christian border guards should refuse to keep anyone out: "If a stranger sojourn with thee in your land, ye shall not vex him. But the stranger that dwelleth with you shall be unto you as one born among you" (Lev 19:33-34).

Given the wonderful publicity Kim Davis has gotten, why aren't more Christians refusing service? Christians could be known as people who refuse to serve others, except for this: "Jesus sat down, and called the twelve, and saith unto them, 'If any desire to be first, the same shall be last of all, and servant of all'" (Mark 9:35).

Donald Trump stole my old church (July 13, 2017)

When I was a high school senior, I became angry with my church. The story of Jesus was leading me away from what they taught me. I wondered if they had read the Bible they kept telling me to read.

Here is a partial list of things I stopped believing: Christians are going to fly up into the sky any minute. The earth is 6,000 years old. Budweiser is the devil's poison. Women are disqualified from telling the Christian story if there is a pulpit in front of them. Gay organists can serve the church only if they are not seen in public with their partners. The pope is the antichrist. My Jewish friends are going to burn in hell forever. Everyone who smokes marijuana should be executed. Kindergarten teachers should carry handguns. Poor people get what they deserve.

I decided that my church was filled with narrow-minded fundamental-
ists who were not worthy of my new enlightened state.

But as time passed, I made peace with the church of my childhood. I
grew more appreciative. They may have taught me a few terrible things, but
they also introduced me to Jesus. I defended them by saying that my old
church was a victim of the culture.

Here is a partial list of the lies I told myself: The people in my old
church are not against women but actually believe they are defending the
family. They sound racist because they are afraid. They appear homophobic
only because they do not know gay people. They will stop being prejudiced against Muslims as soon as they meet Muslims. They defend gun
ownership because they love hunting. Their hostility towards the poor is a
misunderstanding of the American dream.

I convinced myself that while much of what they believe goes against
the teachings of Christ, they are first and foremost Christians at heart. I
was wrong.

Two weeks ago, I went to my parents' Southern Baptist church. I had
not been to a service in that particular church in thirty-five years. The peace
I had made with my childhood church began to fall apart.

The pickups in the parking lot had Trump/Pence bumper stickers.
American flags were in the front yard, at the front of the sanctuary, and
on the front of the order of worship. The congregation sang "God Bless
America," "My Country, 'Tis of Thee," and "Onward, Christian Soldiers."
I heard, "We could use more fire and brimstone," "We finally have a pres-
ident who is doing what needs to be done," and "We have to get rid of
Obamacare right now."

Eighty-seven percent of my parents' church-filled county in Mississippi
voted for Trump. Donald Trump has made it obvious that my old church
is not filled with followers of Christ. You cannot follow Jesus and support
a tax cut for the rich that would end health care to millions of the oldest,
poorest, and sickest people. You cannot follow Jesus and hate minorities.
You cannot follow Jesus and treat women as inferior.

When faced with the choice of following Christ by caring for the
hungry or supporting a politician who promises to make the rich richer,
my old church ignores the faith they profess. When given the opportunity
to extend hospitality to refugees, my old church chooses bigotry. When
responding to a dishonest president, my old church defends the lies.

I have come to the painful realization that God is not the point of
my old church. My old church is shaped more by Fox News than Jesus'
Good News. My old church is a chaplain to nationalism, patriarchy, and

nostalgia. My old church is the enemy of the environment, science, and equality.

I am not going to defend my old church anymore. If you are acting like a racist, homophobe, or misogynist in 2017, then you are a racist, homophobe, or misogynist.

How can anyone think that a church that supports Trump is what Jesus had in mind?

St. Augustine said, "The church is a whore, but she is my mother." My mother church is sleeping with Donald Trump.

Trump is lying; we have to keep listening (August 10, 2017)

We cannot live in community if lies carry the same weight as truth, if bad words are allowed to destroy good ones. We cannot get used to the president's lies. We cannot accept alternative facts. We cannot stop insisting on honesty.

Lots of people who have the Ten Commandments hanging on their wall are tempted to ignore the ninth one, but we have to keep paying attention. Presidents have been dishonest for a long time, but it has always been our job to hold them accountable. Our work is harder now because no president of either party has ever had so little regard for reality. Presidents need to get in trouble when they lie.

Trump lies about the tremendous size of his electoral victory, the amazing number of people at his inauguration, and the huge number of times he has been on the cover of *Time*. He lies about health care, voter fraud, wiretapping, his tax returns, trade deficits, vetting for immigrants, terror attacks in Sweden, and a nonexistent apology from *The New York Times*. He lies about things that are easily checked—like a nonexistent phone call from Mexico's president calling to praise Trump's immigration policy.

If Donald Trump had been our first president, he would claim that the cherry tree is still standing while holding an ax and eating cherries. Kellyanne Conway would roll her eyes and back him up.

We cannot say, "That's Trump being Trump." We cannot believe that truth does not matter because truth is bigger than the presidency.

Last week, the president said, "I got a call from the head of the Boy Scouts saying that it was the greatest speech that was ever made to them." The greatest speech began with, "Who the hell wants to speak about politics when I'm in front of the Boy Scouts?" and then answered the question.

In the greatest speech, Trump called Washington a "sewer" to an audience of Scouts who began making fart noises. The leaders of the Boy Scouts say that none of them called the president to tell him how great the speech was.

Sarah Huckabee Sanders, who misses Sean Spicer more than she thought she would, explained that Trump did not actually take a phone call—as Trump said—but had a conversation. Her defense made the news for a day.

But this Sanders quote is being ignored: "I saw nothing but roughly 40,000 to 45,000 Boy Scouts cheering the president on throughout his remarks and I think they were pretty excited that he was there."

Boy Scouts need to cheer the president. Boy Scouts need to admire the president. Boy Scouts need to believe the president. Trump's lies are a big deal when young people cheer for a leader who does not care about honesty.

Conventional wisdom is that the lies are hurting Trump and his policies, but the truth is that lies set everyone's pants on fire. Trump may have been elected president not in spite of his lies but because of them. His presidency may be the result of our lack of integrity.

We have to understand that justice depends on people telling the truth. Lies are matches that destroy forests that have been growing for decades. Lies turn harmony into hatred. Lies makes us forget how good honesty is.

Mahatma Gandhi said, "There is no God higher than truth." Lying hurts everyone by distancing us from the higher truth. When our leaders love partisan politics more than truth, the whole country loses its way.

We need to be indignant when the president lies. We cannot let untruths pass unchallenged without damage to our souls. We need to defend truth because truth is our best defense.

The words we hear affect our hearts—even when we wish they did not. We are what we hear. We need leaders who know how to bless us with what they say. We need words that heal. We need words that make us better.

We need to make America honest again.

Entitlement: One more reason Brett Kavanaugh is unqualified to sit on the Supreme Court (October 2, 2018)

In a nonresponse to a question from Senator Mazie Keiko Hirono of Hawaii, U.S. Supreme Court nominee Brett Kavanaugh said, "I got into Yale Law School. That's the number one law school in the country. I had no connections there. I got there by busting my tail in college."

If this statement reflects what he believes, then Brett Kavanaugh is not qualified to be on the Supreme Court. A Supreme Court justice has to recognize that there are many smart, hard-working people who do not get to go to Yale. Kavanaugh probably did study hard, and workouts at Tobin's house must have been strenuous, but it is stunning that he would claim that he went to Yale with "no connections."

Kavanaugh should know that many intelligent, industrious people do not have two parents who are lawyers—one a Circuit Court Judge—and a grandfather who went to Yale. Most cannot afford a private high school where the tuition is $60,280 a year. Many high school campuses are not 93 acres. None of the public high schools in my area have an eleven-lane swimming pool with a diving area. Kavanaugh may be surprised to learn that not all high schools have their own nine-hole golf course. (Associate Justice Neil Gorsuch, by the way, is also a Georgetown Prep graduate, class of 1985, so perhaps we could argue that some other high school could be represented on the Supreme Court.)

Kavanaugh's experience at an elite prep school, an elite college, and an elite law school is not normal. Some teenagers cannot go to workouts after school because they have to go to work after school to help their family pay the bills. Many do not have beach houses. Most never belong to a fraternity. When Kavanaugh said of Christine Blasey Ford, "She and I did not travel in the same social circles," was it a defense or an insult?

Wealth and privilege do not exclude someone from the Supreme Court, but not recognizing the advantages one has been given should be disqualifying. Kavanaugh kept saying, "I worked my tail off." Judges can be proud of their education, but they have to understand that what they have been given is not available to most.

Some privileged people desperately want to believe that they deserve everything they have. Kavanaugh gives the impression that he feels entitled. He expresses anger more easily than sympathy. Kavanaugh's demeanor suggests that he would find it hard to empathize with a pregnant teenager, a homeless veteran, or a refugee from El Salvador.

Judges have to listen carefully to victims of systems that have profited the judges. Interpreting the law is an act of imagination as well as reason. Good judges see beyond their own perspectives and life experience.

Justices have to empathize with victims of sexual assault, partner violence, and other misogynistic behavior. Justices have to care about girls and women facing unwanted pregnancies. Justices cannot make judgments that will affect the economically disadvantaged without understanding the terrible costs of poverty.

The best judges imagine what it is like for people of color afraid to walk in a white neighborhood, gay people unwelcomed in certain businesses, and college students clinging to DACA. The best judges see faces as well as cases.

Good lawyers can grow up in a society that offers preference to rich white men, but the privileged have to recognize their privilege. On September 7, 2018, during the first round of his confirmation hearing, Kavanaugh said the court should not be a partisan body. He was right. Judges cannot favor the wealthy over the vulnerable.

The best of those born to privilege recognize their privilege as a gift to be shared. President Trump needs to find a nominee who can imagine what life is like for those who know that no matter how smart they are or how hard they work, they will never go to Yale. Entitled people have enough representation on the Supreme Court.

Christian flag breaking (July 14, 2015)

An excited patriot handed me one of those 10-inch flags that you stick into your lawn on July 4. The plastic red, white, and blue was intact, but the pole that once held it together was broken three stripes from the top. I did not ask for an unbroken one. I do not like flags.

I grew up in small towns in Mississippi where Confederate flags flew in front of church-sponsored all-white private schools. When I became the pastor of a country church, I hid the American flag in the basement, but it miraculously made its way back to the sanctuary in time for Vacation Bible School. The children pledged to "the republic for which it stands" as well as to the Christian flag "and the kingdom for which it stands." The words ran together.

We saluted these flags because everyone on our side saluted these flags. No matter how much well-meaning people want to pretend otherwise, flags say, "I am this, and if you're not, then you can go to hell." If you do not think that is true, try to imagine an Alabama fan with an Auburn flag on the pickup truck, a U.S. presidential candidate wearing an Iraqi flag lapel pin, or the Mexican flag flying over Trump Tower. Half the point of a flag is to let people know they are *not* part of the group.

Rudyard Kipling's poem "*We and They*" closes with a stanza that could have been about flags:

All good people agree,
and all good people say,
All nice people, like Us, are We

and everyone else is They
But if you cross over the sea,
instead of over the way,
You may end by (think of it!) looking on We
as only a sort of They!

I do not like flags, except for the broken one I was given. The broken flag says that we, like they, are not all we should be. The broken flag has lost its sense of superiority. The broken flag says, "I am cracked, wrecked, smashed, shattered, and fragmented, just like whatever I might represent."

The broken flag is contrite. We should break all our flags—maybe three stripes from the top. Breaking our flags would turn a symbol of power into an act of repentance. The pledge to a broken flag might include a more honest "not with liberty and justice for all, but with that hope calling us to change." We could skip "one nation under God," which must make God's eyes roll anyway.

We should make flags with flaws, like Navajo weavers who put an imperfection in each rug as a "Spirit line," a break in the border to allow the Spirit to be free and a reminder that all of creation is flawed.

On July 10, 2015, South Carolina took down the Confederate flag from the Capitol grounds in Columbia because that flag is more than broken; it is evil beyond reclaiming. What makes me pause is that, as the color guard removed the flag, the crowd chanted "U.S.A." as though the hockey team had just beaten the Russians. This occasion to confess the racism that pervades our country may have been, for some, yet another moment of triumphalism, us defeating them.

The United States Flag Code states that when a flag is worn or damaged, it should "be destroyed in a dignified way, preferably by burning." Directions are given on how to fold the flag and how big the fire should be, and with the suggestion to recite the Pledge of Allegiance as the flag burns.

Instead of disposing of torn and tattered flags, we should run them up the flagpole and see who salutes. The broken flags are the ones we need to keep.

Preaching peace in a timid church (March 11, 2013)

When ministers are afraid to speak prophetically about peace, they fail to be a voice for the Prince of Peace.

At the 2012 William Self Preaching Lectures at the McAfee School of Theology, "Preaching Peace in a Crumbling Empire," Brian McLaren argued that the Bible is a call to speak God's word of peace to an empire built on power.

"We preach the peace of one who was crucified, so we cannot preach power that crucifies," McLaren said. "We preach a way of love and service, so we cannot preach conquest and domination."

McLaren's words in the chapel were challenging and inspiring. The words in the hall—not so much. Popular opinion seems to be that peace belongs in lectures but not in sermons:

"That peace stuff wouldn't fly at my church."
"Now we know why McLaren isn't a pastor anymore."
"His last church must have been in Switzerland."
"If I preach on peace, war will break out in the next deacons' meeting."
"I'll preach against the war when McLaren agrees to pay my kid's college tuition."

In Jesus' day, prophets were run out of town, thrown off a cliff, or stoned in the middle of the village. Now we dismiss prophets in the conversations between lectures.

When did peace become a peripheral issue? How can ministers read the Gospels and think peace is an optional topic? When Jesus preached, "Blessed are the peacemakers," he included preachers. Would the one who commanded us to "love our enemies" think we do enough to stop killing our enemies?

The church has become reticent to preach on war and peace. During the Vietnam War, preachers like Martin Luther King Jr. and William Sloane Coffin were well known for speaking prophetically against the war. Why weren't there similarly well-known prophetic voices during the war in Iraq? If Christians never hear a sermon on peacemaking, will they assume that faith has nothing to do with the most important issues of our day? Will they get the impression that God has no concern about the war in Afghanistan?

Ministers are not exempt from preaching peace because it will be uncomfortable, the finance committee will not be happy, or the inbox will fill up on Monday morning. The United States has amassed the most formidable weapons systems the world has seen.

Our military spending is equal to that of the rest of the world put together. The combined military budget of Iran, North Korea, Cuba, and Syria is less than 4 percent of our budget. The U.S. planned military spending in 2012 is $671 billion while China's budget is $106 billion.

Courageous preachers speak to the cost of war, the present wars, the next war, the shedding of blood, the wasting of innocent life, the demeaning of people, the destruction of property, the poverty that results, and the hatred that poisons.

When war is portrayed by politicians as the less painful option, ministers need to persistently speak the hope of peace. Killing terrorists will not defeat terrorism. Preemptive wars do not make us safer. Crushing a few despots perpetuates hatred. War on Islamic countries ultimately increases the number of Islamic terrorists.

If the U.S. supported a policy based more on human rights, international law, and sustainable development for poor countries and less on arms transfers and military attacks, we would be safer.

Our national security must be based on more than military power. We should preach in support of diplomacy, economic development, and the protection of human rights. We should recognize that poverty and national humiliation are as dangerous to our security as any weapon. We need to return to the most effective ways America has influenced nations throughout the world, by offering a helping hand and abiding by our deepest principles.

When ministers are afraid to speak prophetically about peace, they fail to be a voice for the Prince of Peace. They have ceased to be ministers of the Gospel of Jesus Christ. Christian preachers proclaim Christ's different, better way—even when it is hard.

What you should preach if Donald comes to your church (April 1, 2019)

On St. Patrick's Day, Donald Trump made a surprise visit to St. John's Episcopal Church, two blocks from the White House. The interim rector, Reverend Bruce McPherson, must have been warned because he delivered a pointed message. According to CNN, he called on worshipers to stand against the "hateful rhetoric" that spurred a gunman in Christchurch, New Zealand, to open fire on mosques two days earlier, killing fifty worshipers and wounding another fifty. (The alleged shooter called himself a Trump supporter.)

McPherson called the incident "one more gratuitous attack on innocent people at worship" and asked, "What can we do? Well, perhaps we're called whenever we overhear hateful slurs against other people. Perhaps we need the holy courage to call them out because that's just not us. It's not easy to confront someone. It takes courage, I know. But it's up to us. Courage is contagious. And acting courageously especially in light of speech like that catches on and spreads."

McPherson's strong sermon is a reminder that ministers need to be prepared. We need to have a regular sermon ready for each Sunday. But for our own spiritual health we also need an if-Donald-Trump-happens-to-show-up sermon.

Some ministers—particularly mainline Protestants—dream of seeing the president slide into a pew during the opening hymn. If we ever get the chance, we will seize the opportunity to speak truth to power. We will let loose bravely like the prophets we long to be. We will speak fearlessly for the powerless—children, immigrants, and the poor. We will prophesy boldly against the evils of ignoring climate change and dismantling health care. We will thunder courageously against materialism, militarism, nationalism, racism, sexism, gun violence, Islamophobia, and homophobia.

After hearing McPherson's powerful sermon against "hateful rhetoric" on March 17, the president went back to the White House and—throughout that very afternoon and evening—tweeted negative comments about CNN, NPR, Democrats, General Motors, Robert Mueller, Christopher Steele, Hillary Clinton, Ilhan Omar, and Meghan McCain.

Letting the president have it for all the ways we think he falls short is not going to work the way ministers like me want it to. We are not going to convince Donald Trump or his followers that his positions are wrong with louder, more forceful pronouncements.

I feel as compelled as many of my clergy colleagues to point out the ways in which Trump's actions are antithetical to the Gospel—and we need angry prophets—but anger cannot be everything that Trump's backers hear from us.

Ministers would be better off, at times, asking the Spirit to help the president and his defenders understand that God loves all people. If Donald Trump shows up at your church, tell him about God's mercy. Tell the president that God's grace is bigger than our need for approval, bigger than our sins, and bigger than anything we can ever do. Tell him, "God loves and believes in you."

We should preach the good news of the example we see in Jesus and the hope we see in God. Preaching about anyone's foolishness tends to become less loving than preaching about God's goodness. God's forgiveness is deeper than our brokenness. God's dreams for us are better than we have envisioned.

What would happen if the president really believed in God's love? Trump could have the most surprising third act in the history of politics. What if God's grace took hold of Trump and he started working for the good of those who most need help? Imagine how much fun it would be to see Trump's supporters (including many who stand behind a pulpit every week) have to deal with the president caring for people they have demonized and marginalized. Imagine how much fun it would be to watch Trump's opponents try to figure out how to campaign against a president whose policies were suddenly more generous than their own.

Many of us find it hard to believe that God could change the president of the United States of America. That says as much about us as about Donald Trump. God invites all kinds of ministers to give up anything that sounds like "hateful rhetoric" and preach the power of God's love.

Hungering for a Christian response to Mississippi's veggie burger ban (July 10, 2019)

Right now someone in Mississippi, typing an announcement about the church cookout, is being forced to take a controversial stand. Does the church follow the new state law or continue to serve "veggie burgers"?

How many churches will have the courage to throw a 'shroom burger on the grill? How many congregations will be torn apart by this divisive issue?

Mississippi lawmakers recently ended their long, statewide nightmare by banning the marketing of "veggie burgers." They say the law will put an end to the unfortunate incidents that have ruined the lives of carnivorous consumers who have accidentally tasted tofu. Their argument centers on the thought-provoking question: Why do the makers of these "burgers" become vegan if the first thing they do is make them look and taste like meat?

Lawsuits from vegetarian-friendly groups are trying to overturn the restrictions on the use of meat-related terms for plant-based foods. The lawsuit denounces "meat label censorship" and claims, "The ban serves only to create consumer confusion where none previously existed."

It is no longer enough for a label to say "100 percent vegan." The law, which was passed in March and took effect on July 1, protects meat products (like hamburgers) from being mistaken for plant-based alternatives (like veggie burgers) by barring the use of the term "burger" to refer to veggie burgers. Perpetrators can go to prison—taken away in a patty wagon—for printing the words "veggie burger."

Prisoner 1: "I robbed a bank. What are you in for?"

Carl Jr.: "I called a burger a Veg-It Thickburger."

Is this a real problem? Is the phrase "veggie burger" unclear? Haven't we been calling them veggie, vegan, and tofu burgers for decades?

Are people going to grocery stores, picking up veggie burgers without reading the label, throwing them on the grill, and biting into them before realizing they are eating vegan fare? God forbid a Mississippi resident, thinking they are eating highly processed meat filled with cancer-causing nitrates, should unwittingly taste a plant-based burger. No one wants to be tricked into a healthier option.

This is complicated. What happens when food scientists come up with cell-based meat products which are identical to meat from animals but grown from stem cells in a factory? Will Jon Hamm and Kevin Bacon have to change their names? Did they consider going further and saying the term "burger" can only be applied to a grilled patty sandwich made in the traditional method within the Hamburg region of Germany? What about calling it a "plantwich" or "planturger"? Or, as a nod to presidential spelling, "hamberder"?

Do people who buy a burger labeled "veggie burger" thinking it comes from a cow have a right to feel misled? Are reasonable consumers deceived by "meatless steaks" and "vegan jerky"? This law raises difficult questions for legislators concerned that hamburgers are not ham, hot dogs are not dogs, circus peanuts are not peanuts, Buffalo wings are not buffalo, and refried beans are not fried twice. What about almond milk?

A cynical person might think the meat industry wants to stifle competition. The Mississippi Cattlemen's Association, which pushed for the new law, seems to have more political influence than vegans in Mississippi. The state is run by the party of small government, but being a vegetarian is as un-American as reducing gun violence.

Churches afraid to bite into the veggie burger issue could divert attention by pointing out a long list of problems bigger than lentil burgers that Mississippi lawmakers might have addressed. The state is ranked near the bottom in terms of poverty, high school graduation rates, infant mortality, racial conflict, and obesity (which makes the new law ironic as well as silly). Arguing over what to call a plant-based burger should not be a legislative priority.

The church should see this as an opportunity to be courageous. Christians could protect the marginalized by defending "meatless meatballs," "vegan bacon," and "beefless burgers." How amazing would it be if Mississippi prisons were overrun with church people who put "veggie burgers" on the Wednesday night supper menu? How surprising would it be if a church put "Vegetarians are welcome" on the marquee?

Or maybe this story is a total nothingburger. Can I say that?

Gun Violence

A long, hard way to reduce gun violence (December 14, 2017)

After the next person opens fire in a room full of innocent people and after we have gathered to read the names of the victims, grieve for the families of those who died, and encourage people to work for common-sense gun laws, we need to talk about a long, hard way that we can be part of the solution.

The ability of individuals to inflict suffering has stunned us. The men who commit these horrific acts have a staggering lack of empathy. The background story that keeps repeating itself is of a loner detached from the community turned into a shooter. These isolated individuals are susceptible to being radicalized online by groups spewing racial hatred, nationalistic propaganda, and narcissistic notions of going out in a blaze of "glory." Some have committed murder out of loyalty to groups they have never met.

Shooters are not born wanting to destroy others. They have been taught to hate. If we can teach one another to kill, we can teach one another to love. We need communities that invite people out of isolation.

I saw him in a small church in Mississippi. He fought in Vietnam and came back messed up. He limped and took painkillers that doctors did not prescribe. He looked a foot to your right during conversations. The less he knew about a subject the more he talked. His volume was inversely proportional to the importance of what he said. His wardrobe was army surplus before there were army surplus stores. He was not allowed to drive.

When he first came back from the war, he moved in with his parents. They soon told him to move on and stay away. His army pension and odd jobs were enough for him to get by.

The veteran had no friends—except for his church. A rotation of people brought him to church on Sundays. He often interrupted worship by shouting, "What song was that?" The pianist got used to it.

When the congregation shook his hand or gave him a hug, it was the most human contact he'd had since the previous Sunday. The potluck dinners were the best meals he ate, and he took home leftovers. People called during the week to ask if he was OK. They helped him get the mental health care he needed. He was difficult, but the church never asked him to move on and stay away.

The church of my childhood had big problems—racism, sexism, and homophobia—but, at their best, they were family for those who had no family. They cared for some who would not have been cared for otherwise. This happens in thousands of congregations.

Religious people have committed terrible acts of violence, but people who feel loved are less likely to hurt others. People who have been taught compassion are less likely to open fire with semi-automatic rifles. Caring for broken people can be scary, but not caring for them can be dangerous, too.

Houses of worship need to reach out to those who are difficult to love. Children, in particular, need to be taught the value of a caring community. The lonely need a place to be heard.

Those who are not part of a religious congregation need to provide ways for those who feel unconnected to be part of a group. Community organizations offer shared purposes that are bigger than the individual. We need to bring people together to talk face to face.

In our current political climate, loving one another sounds not only naïve but also like an act of defiance. Our president speaks out of anger in the face of violence. We have to remind one another that compassion is not weakness, and arrogance is not strength. The culture that does not care for the broken will be a violent culture.

One of the long-term solutions to gun violence is a sense of community. We will always be in danger as long as some feel like they have been told to move on and stay away.

"Stand and Fight" or "Sit and Talk"?
(May 11, 2017)

As we drive to my parents' house, we see that the neighbors have a big sign in the yard: "NRA, Stand and Fight." A normal yard sign in that part of the country might be "Congratulations Class of 2017" or "Bitter Divorce Sale." I am suddenly self-conscious about our New York license plate. "Stand and Fight" is less welcoming than "No Soliciting Unless You Are Selling Thin Mints."

The sign does not explain who they hope to fight. The word "rifle" suggests they are not aiming for thoughtful conversation. Who do they want to fight?

Maybe the sign is meant to frighten potential thieves, like the sign that reads "Protected by ADT Security Systems." (Full disclosure: We bought a house with one of those signs by the front door and left it there for seven years. We did not pay for a security system.)

Maybe they are worried about foreign invaders. "Stand and Fight" might be a more subtle version of "Protected by Smith & Wesson." Most will be surprised if terrorists are discovered in Itawamba County. (The newspaper lists police calls that often include cows wandering on to the road.)

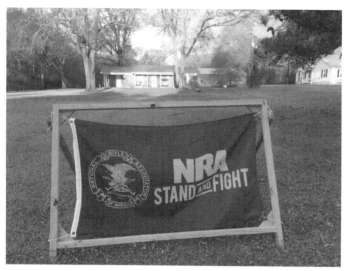

NRA Version of a Welcome Mat?

Maybe I am the one they want to fight. They may not care for people who believe there is room for improvement in our gun laws. I continue to think there is common ground between people of good will in favor of increased safety and people of good will who love the Second Amendment.

We can strengthen background checks. We can do more to keep guns out of the hands of felons, domestic abusers, and the mentally ill. We can push for reasonable waiting periods. We can promote smart technology that senses fingerprints. We can require safeties that lower the number of accidental shootings. We can find sensible ways to keep guns off college campuses, where gun-related suicides are increasing. We can restrict magazine capacity on assault rifles. We can work to ban automatic weapons that have no purpose other than mass shootings. We can make murdering another human being more cumbersome.

Unfortunately, "Stand and Fight" could be interpreted to mean that the way to end conversations about gun laws is to shoot the people who want gun laws. I may have this completely wrong. The one who put up the sign may be a reflective person with whom I could share a helpful exchange of ideas, but most of us are reticent to engage someone who begins with "Stand and Fight."

I checked the NRA website but could not find an explanation for the "Stand and Fight" yard sign. I did learn that you can purchase NRA portable target stands, concealed carry handbags, and concealment leggings.

I asked my parents about the people who live in the house with the sign. They are renting the house from one of our distant relatives. (The street is named for my great-grandfather. Everyone in town is a distant relative.) The sign, which probably belongs to my relative, went up the day after the election in November, replacing a "Vote for Trump" sign that was not necessary in Mississippi.

I decided to take a photograph in case I thought of anything to write about the sign. Standing in their yard with my cell phone was awkward. How would I explain myself if someone questioned my presence on their lawn? What if they brought a rifle to the discussion?

I came up with several excuses:

"I am a surveyor who forgot to bring my surveying stuff."

"My second cousin used to live here." (This is true.)

"I too am a proud member of the NRA. I want to join the fight. Who are we fighting?"

I took the picture without incident, but then the story took a surprising turn. The next day the sign was gone. The timing may have been a coincidence. Or maybe not.

Perhaps the conversation went like this:

"Honey, there's a man on the lawn taking a picture of our sign."

"Why would anybody take a picture of our sign?"

"Maybe he's a surveyor."

"A surveyor with a cell phone?"

"Maybe he's a fellow member of the NRA who believes in the Second Amendment."

"Have you thought about whether 'Stand and Fight' is the best way to express our openness to others' ideas? It could be interpreted negatively."

"Still, I would hope someone would talk to us before they publish a picture of our yard."

"What if we put up a more helpful sign? Let's look for one that says 'Sit and Talk.'"

Putting an end to prayer vigils (November 24, 2016)

Jewish synagogues have been defaced with swastikas. Latina women have been threatened. Muslim women have been forced to remove their hijabs. On Veterans Day, Marie Boyle, a U.S. army veteran from the Philippines, was told to "Go back to Mexico."

I do not want to go to another vigil. Sometime soon someone will easily obtain a gun that no hunter would ever use. He will open fire in a room full of innocent people.

Clergy will organize a vigil where we read the names of the victims. We will grieve for the families of those who died. We will read Scripture. We will pray for an end to gun violence.

We will give anyone paying careful attention the impression that we are not sure that God and God's people working together can stop or even slow gun violence. The ministers will not offer concrete suggestions as to how we might prevent the next tragedy. The ministers will either be afraid of offending someone or they will not know what to suggest. Does a prayer vigil that leads to no action make us complicit?

The temptation right now for those who have worked against the easy availability of guns is, if not to give up, to stop trying so hard. But this is not the time to—as one of my dear friends put it—binge-watch *The West Wing* and eat ice cream. This is the time to be vigilant.

This is the time to work to make it harder to die from gun violence. More than thirty people in our nation are murdered by guns on an average day.

Gun violence is a domestic violence problem. In an average month, 51 women are shot to death by a current or former husband or boyfriend.

Gun violence is a child abuse problem. The number of children and teens killed by guns in one year would fill 126 classrooms of 20 students each.

Gun violence is a mental health problem. There are 21,000 suicides committed using guns each year.

Gun violence is a safety problem. More than 45 people are shot accidentally each day. (Statistics are from faithinpubliclife.org, everytown.org, and childrensdefense.org.)

Gun violence is a faith problem. Christians have to be broken-hearted by the gun deaths in our country. We have to be more concerned with the Sixth Commandment than the Second Amendment. We may want to say that gun violence is as prevalent as it is because politicians are afraid of losing their jobs, but it is also true that Christians have not worked as we should to end the violence. We cannot pretend we cannot do anything.

We can work to strengthen background checks. Forty percent of the guns sold legally in the United States are bought without a background check. No records are kept. No questions are asked. Criminals buy guns online from unlicensed sellers.

We can insist that background check laws work. Connecticut improved their background check laws and cut gun deaths by 40 percent. Missouri repealed their background check laws and gun deaths increased by 40 percent. Common sense demands we keep guns out of the hands of felons, domestic abusers, and those adjudicated as mentally ill. We can regulate guns as closely as we do cars.

We can require locks that make it harder to pull a trigger and lower the number of accidental shootings. We can work to ban the automatic weapons that seem to have no purpose other than mass shootings.

Christians disagree on how best to address the epidemic of gun violence, but we cannot disagree on the tragic nature of gun violence. We have to do something. Support courageous politicians. Complain about the ones who are not courageous. Speak up for commonsense gun laws that make our streets and sanctuaries safe. Defend the right of families to walk their neighborhoods without the risk of being shot.

Pray for an end to prayer vigils. Pray for the time when we have no list of victims' names to read. Pray that we will have the courage to speak up. Pray that we will realize that, especially in hard times, God expects more from us.

Religious terrorism (January 22, 2016)

I belong to a religious group that has been responsible for horrible acts of terrorism. The majority of us do not believe these terrorists are being true to our faith, but others insist on painting us all with the same brush. Religions that include terrorists are having a hard time, but I hope those with different religious heritages will treat us fairly.

Do not judge our holy book by a few stories. Lots of people condemn sacred texts without having read the book, but the Bible's violent stories do not characterize the whole text. Yes, when some boys call one of God's prophets "Baldy," Elisha curses them in the name of the Lord and calls two bears to maul forty-two children. God commands the Israelites to destroy all the women, children, infants, cattle, sheep, and donkeys among the Amalekites. The prophet Hosea promises that God will take revenge against Samaria and "their little ones shall be dashed to pieces and their pregnant women ripped open." Some argue that a sacred text with such terrible stories leads its followers to be violent, but do not judge the Bible by a few passages.

Do not condemn Christianity for our most embarrassing moments. Some evaluate entire religions by the worst events in their history. This is unfortunate because Christianity has a history of terrorism. The Crusades were a series of military campaigns sanctioned by various popes in the Middle Ages. We want to think Christians are getting better, but the evidence is shaky. In 2012, Wade Michael Page killed six people in a Sikh temple in Oak Creek, Wisconsin, because he believed he was preserving Christian society. The Army of God, a loose network of Christians, has a history of terrorist attacks on abortion providers. Last summer, church attender Dylann Roof murdered nine people at Emanuel African Methodist Episcopal Church in Charleston, South Carolina. The stewardess who refuses to give a Christian an unopened soda can for fear he will use it as a weapon may be genuinely afraid, but we hope you do not give in to this kind of bigotry. Christian terrorism makes it easy to dismiss us as violent people, but it is not fair.

Do not judge Christianity by those who give us a bad name. Disparaging a religion because of its worst adherents is wrong, but many point out that Hitler grew up Catholic and talked about "divine providence." Pat Robertson called for the destruction of Islam and all its followers. The president of Liberty University, Jerry Falwell Jr., encouraged students to buy guns to "end those Muslims" who might threaten them. Jim Jones, Fred Phelps, and David Koresh are not who most Christians are, so do not judge Christianity by its most terrible members.

Do not attack Christianity for political gain. Some politician in some country may pander for votes by calling for a ban on Christian immigration, but do not give in to narrow-mindedness. Many Christian refugees are running for their lives. Do not listen to anyone who says an immigration policy that includes Christians is "importing terrorism."

Do not judge us by our clothing. Many Christians wear what are called "Christian T-shirts" that proclaim messages like these:

Salvation makes everything better. Just like bacon.
I lost faith in humanity before it was cool.
White Straight Conservative Christian: How else may I offend you today?

Those who are not Christians see this kind of clothing—not to mention WWJD bracelets—as a refusal to fit in: "Why can't they dress like everyone else?" The outfits may seem odd and offensive but treat people in Christian clothing with the same respect you would give someone in a Jewish yarmulke or a Muslim hijab.

As it says in the Koran, "Had God willed, he would have made you a single community, but he wanted to test you regarding what has come to you. So compete with each other in doing good. Every one of you will return to God and he will inform you regarding the things about which you differed" (Surat al-Ma'ida, 48).

Churches should be more like grand juries—except for the judging part (September 20, 2019)

They made it clear that if I ever mention a defendant's name, a witness's story or a lawyer's hair color I will spend the rest of my life in a windowless room begging for bread and water. They told us about a juror who posted a picture of a witness on Facebook. That juror will be the last one out of Guantanamo.

I recently spent two weeks on a grand jury dealing with 21 cases that I cannot talk about. We were allowed to take notes, but could not take them home. I wrote things that would make you laugh out loud and break your heart, but those amusing, tear-jerking notes have been destroyed.

When you hear the marshal call your name the first time it is alarming: "Congratulations, Mr. Younger, you're the foreperson. There's no judge in a grand jury courtroom, so you sit in the judge's seat, swear in the witnesses and lead the deliberations."

"Was I chosen at random?"

"We picked you because of your age and occupation."

I understand why they want old referees, but am surprised that they recognize that ministers know all about officiating arguments.

If you are ever fortunate enough to be on a grand jury, you want to be the foreperson. Because there is no defendant, defense attorney or judge, some witnesses mistook me for someone with authority. When anyone asked permission to do anything I always replied, "I'll allow it." I found this amusing, though one attorney said, "Stop doing that."

I decided my job was to lighten the mood during deliberations:

"Do we agree that we have sufficient evidence that the defendant is not a criminal mastermind?"

"Let me remind you that nothing I say has any probative value." (You had to be there.)

"I have reasonable cause to believe we should go to lunch."

The twenty-three of us enjoyed each other's company. The jury checked just about every box on the ethnicity questionnaire. We were uneducated, overeducated, unemployed and overemployed. We had a variety of viewpoints on politics and the New York Yankees.

We talked compassionately about victims, our complex feelings about law enforcement and the way race complicates everything. We learned that if you are arrested for stealing and are shown a videotape of the event, you should not shout, "That's me!"

We listened to people who have been robbed, beaten and shot. We heard about people who think their best option is to sell drugs from a basement apartment, and that it makes sense to take a gun to a barbecue. These people have hard lives.

I decided that if no one asked my occupation I would not tell them, but at the end of the first week, after I quoted Atticus Finch without giving him credit, a member of the jury asked, "Are you planning to go to law school?"

I said, "I don't think I need to quit my day job just yet."

"What is your day job?"

I thought about questioning the relevance of the question, but told the truth: "I'm a minister."

The jury stopped deliberating. The conversation slowed. In that setting, being a minister got in the way of being a friend. The camaraderie was gone for those who have not experienced the church at its best.

Why doesn't everyone say, "I'm so glad to hear that you're a minister, because the church has always been a source of hope for me and my family"? Sometimes churches do not offer comfort. Most churches are not as inclusive as they want to believe.

We spent two weeks listening to stories that make it clear the world needs good churches. There are too many battered, hopeless and frightened people and too many angry, unloved and mean people.

We need churches that ask hard questions: What can the church do for women who have been beaten by their boyfriends? How should the church care for the cashier who is stealing money to pay the electric bill? How should the church respond to those who drive drunk? How can the church be honest about the racism that has infiltrated our communities of faith? Does the church worry about what God worries about, weep over what God weeps over and love those God loves? What would happen if the church asked broken people, "What kind of church do you need?"

We have enough churches that keep their distance from shattered lives, do only what is expected and exist to maintain the church. We need churches that proclaim release to the captives, care for the victims and become family to those who need a family.

I do not get to serve on another jury for eight years, but I have been given sufficient evidence that churches need to figure out how to become friends with victims, change the lives of offenders and listen to the broken-hearted.

Hope is present but elusive. Look harder. (October 12, 2017)

The October 1 gun massacre in Las Vegas is devastating, but will anyone be surprised if churches are planning another prayer vigil in a month? When the NRA came out in favor of restricting bump stocks—the device that makes semi-automatic weapons act like automatic weapons—I thought it was a hopeful change. Then I learned that bump stocks are one of the few items related to guns on which the NRA makes no money. They are not thinking about human lives. They are still thinking about money.

The reaction to Hurricane Maria turned a disaster in which thirty-four people died into a story about racism. The generosity of those who rushed to Puerto Rico to help got less attention than the suspicion that the official responses to Harvey and Irma were more rapid because more white Americans were affected. Also lost was the much-needed conversation about how climate change is contributing to tropical storms.

The supreme leader of North Korea is unbalanced and unhinged. Our leader has responded by threatening to "totally destroy North Korea." Shouldn't we be more shocked when the president threatens to kill 24 million people? Trying to look tough cannot be more important than avoiding a war that takes innocent lives.

Many of us are exhausted, sad, and angry. We do not need the power of positive thinking or Pollyanna optimism. We need strength. We need hope. We need God.

When the world is hard, we have to look harder. We are detectives searching for clues. Hope does not shout, but, if we listen carefully, we hear whispers. Hopeful things are happening, but we have to pay attention. This week:

• A child in California gave a firefighter a hug.
• A congressperson had second thoughts about assault rifles.
• A relief worker in Puerto Rico handed a bottle of water to someone who was thirsty. He did not throw paper towels.

- A diplomat from North Korea and a diplomat from the United States shared a pizza.
- A sixty-year-old ordered his morning coffee in Spanish for the first time.
- A white NFL player asked an African American player why he was kneeling during the anthem, and he listened to the response.
- A black judge acquitted a white racist of a false murder charge.
- A white police officer asked a black teenager how the police could be more helpful.
- A Christian minister asked an imam to talk to her church's youth group.
- A senior citizen who has never been to a protest marched in support of immigrants.
- An office manager sent a memo to the CEO pointing out that women are still paid less than men.
- A father who thinks of himself as old school told his gay son how proud he is of him.
- A cashier took a bite of his grilled cheese and then stopped to say grace.
- A homeless veteran went to a church for dinner and a good night's sleep.
- A composer sitting at her piano found the right note. It was C sharp.
- A six-year-old heard the story of the Prodigal Son for the first time.
- A shopper at a car dealership decided to buy a hybrid.
- A neighbor talked to an elderly woman sitting on her porch.
- A first-semester college student fell in love with Emily Dickinson.
- A sophomore changed his major to social work.
- A visitor to an art museum looked at a Cezanne and was grateful.
- An angry man started to make an angry phone call but then hung up.
- A book group picked Anne Lamott for their next author.
- A fan at a Bruce Springsteen concert believed again.
- A scientist who usually watches MSNBC watched Fox News and thought, "I can understand how someone would feel that way."
- A bald man decided that hair is overrated.
- A preschooler learned to tie his shoes.
- A mother gave in and got her eight-year-old a puppy.
- A couple going through a divorce decided to put the children first.
- An architect received a text from an old friend inviting her to lunch.
- A cabdriver picked up a fare in a wheelchair and took her to the grocery store for free.
- A doctor told an artist that she is going to have a baby girl.
- A retired teacher laughed out loud for the first time since his wife's death.

The world's problems are devastating, so we keep looking for hope. We do not need to pretend everything is okay. We need to pay attention to the hope that surrounds us.

Church Talk

Mary and Joseph—and Kevin (December 22, 2016)

Shivering, wet guests file into the fellowship hall. It is cold and raining on the Thursday before Christmas. Two hundred homeless people have come to church for chicken spaghetti.

I pass a marker around my table. We fill out nametags. I try to quickly learn the names—John Henry, Bill, Cornelius, Tom, Kevin, Mary, and Joe.

On a cold night just before Christmas I am sitting with Mary and Joseph. Mary is young and weary. Joseph is bewildered. His jacket is two sizes too big.

Joseph says, "I hate to ask, but do you have twenty-five cents I could use for the bus? I'm a quarter short and too tired to walk."

One of the occupational hazards of being a preacher is that you frequently find yourself in situations that shout, "Here comes a sermon illustration! Don't miss this!"

I imagine that Mary and Joseph are from out of town. They need a place to stay. I know it is too much to hope that Mary is expecting, but that would be so sweet. I am thinking, "If I ever have a column due right before Christmas, I am going to send Baptist News Global the story of Mary and Joseph coming in from the cold, coming to church just before Christmas."

I start asking questions. The story is not the one for which I was hoping. I am disappointed to learn that Mary is not with Joseph. She is with Kevin. Mary has not been with Kevin long and gives the impression that she and Kevin might not make it to Christmas together.

Joseph is looking for a place to stay, but it is because, as he announces to everyone within shouting distance, "A year ago, I went on a drinking binge and my grandmother kicked me out of the house."

The story no longer seems like part of a Christmas column, but Joseph keeps talking. He is in a job-training program that lasts six months. He had not had a drink for five months when, as he put it, "I got too much money in my pocket."

When his caseworker found out what had happened, Joseph was sure that she would kick him out of the program. He was amazed when she gave him another chance.

Joseph is determined that he is not going to let down the one person who still believes in him. It is not the sentimental story for which I was hoping, but it sounds like God might be in it.

God is with us in more ways than we have imagined. God is with us when we sing "*Joy to the World*" with a joy that comes from deep inside, when like the Grinch we find our hearts growing a few sizes, and when the ghosts of Christmas remind us that Tiny Tim does not live that far away.

God is present even in the midst of horrific tragedies, in the care we offer broken people, and in the longing we feel for a world where children are safe.

God is present when we think more about what others have done for us than about what we have done for them, when we move past what the world owes us to what we owe the world, and when we see that other people are just as real as we are.

God is present when we love children who are challenging, when we care for parents who do not want to be parented, and when we do something kind for the ex-spouse without getting credit.

God is present when we cannot think of a reason that anyone would want to be our friend but find our friends are there anyway, when we choose not to offer thinly veiled criticism, and when we laugh—especially when we wondered if we would ever laugh again.

Much of the time, we do not notice that God is here. We are so used to hearing what we expect and remaining deaf to what we most need that it is hard to break the habit. But if we listen with hope, then we may hear God speaking.

Legend has it that when Joan of Arc was on trial, the archbishop began, "Do you claim to hear angels?"

Joan replied, "Why, yes. Don't you?"

The archbishop was amused: "No, I don't."

"What a pity that you are an archbishop and you cannot hear the songs of angels."

What a pity if we hear the story of Christmas and do not recognize that God is with us.

Penitential pancakes: Sin soaked in syrup (March 4, 2019)

My paper plate was not designed to hold syrup, but I covered it with fluffy golden layers drenched in melted butter and soaked in a sweet amber river of maple deliciousness. Whoever decided overeating should be the prelude to penitence was a genius. Why didn't the churches of my youth know about this? Those churches excelled at food-centered faith but somehow missed out on the spiritual implications of pancakes.

Who wouldn't want to belong to a church that confesses sins by eating copious quantities of sugar? How much different would my faith be if I had grown up with a full-blown pancake-racing tradition? How much fuller would my experience of repentance be if I had learned to run while flipping hotcakes? How would it improve the reputation of Christians if every church had these wonderful, ridiculous events? Who wouldn't want to join a group of people running around a gym in their Sunday best with flapjack-laden skillets?

I have attended three years of Pancake Races at Plymouth Church in Brooklyn. Our races, which take place on the Sunday before Lent, include hairnets, oven mitts, spatulas, and aprons. The early races were not particularly competitive. Women ran in heels.

But by 2017, parents felt that the children's races had become dangerous, so the referee decided to slow them down by having participants run backwards. This was a poorly thought-out rule change that was reversed one race later.

In 2018, the women's race got ugly. Elbows flew. A marathon runner pulled a hamstring. She may have been tripped, which might have followed a shove. Some questioned whether the winner's pancake was flipped the requisite number of times.

At this year's extravaganza, we tried to limit the carnage and the chicanery. We made it clear that there would be no hiding pancakes in pockets to replace dropped pancakes. We let spectators know that gambling would not be allowed.

For the most part, we treated the races with the respect they deserve. The competition was fierce, but there were no casualties. There were accusations of PEDs, but no proof. One gridiron gladiator hid the others' aprons but felt bad about it afterwards.

Plymouth Church Pancake Race, 2019

Six centuries ago, churches in England began having pancake lunches on the day before Lent to use up the butter, milk, eggs, sugar, and fat that were forbidden during Lent. On Pancake Tuesday in 1445, a woman in Olney, England—whose name was lost to history but whose influence was not—was so intent on making pancakes that she did not notice the time until she heard the church bell ring. She raced out of the house and down the street to the church still wearing her apron, pancakes still in her frying pan, tossing them to prevent burning.

Women were soon racing through the streets flipping pancakes. The first woman to complete the course, arrive at the church, serve her pancake to the bell ringer, and be kissed by him was declared the winner.

There is not much biblical precedent for pancake races. Cakes were offered in the temple (Exod 29:2), but cakes offered to the "queen of heaven" were idolatrous (Jer 7:18). Well-intentioned interpreters who look for theological meaning in the ingredients are on shaky ground. Some see eggs as a symbol for creation, flour as the staff of life, salt as wholesomeness, and milk as purity. These commentators are trying way too hard.

Experts in dream interpretation say pancakes are spiritual in nature. Dreams of serving pancakes indicate a longing for joy. Dreams of eating pancakes suggest the desire for a closer family. Some associate pancakes with belonging because their grandparents made blueberry buttermilk pancakes.

Shrove Tuesday, the day of preparation for Lent, is more fun than it sounds. "Shrove" means to hear the confession of sins, assure forgiveness, and give spiritual advice. This does not sound like a party, but Fat Tuesday or Mardi Gras does suggest "Let the good times roll!" In Iceland, Pancake

Tuesday is known as Bursting Day—an apt name for a day of stuffing ourselves.

The point of Pancake Tuesday—the one day of the year no one should go to Waffle House—is not to get the partying out of our system before Lent begins. Feast days remind us to live in gratitude. Celebration, reveling in the pleasures of life, helps us pay attention. We need to thank God for the laughter of a good church, the joy of forgiveness, and the taste of pancakes soaked in syrup.

Reading the obituaries for Lent: Reminders that people are often good (March 8, 2018)

Some Christians stop eating meat for Lent. Some give up Facebook. Some read the Psalms. When I was a young minister in Indiana, I began reading the obituaries for Lent. The *Paoli News-Republican* came out on Tuesday and Friday. A normal edition included two or three obituaries that were written by the newspaper's staff. No family was ever charged for an obituary.

The writers interviewed the deceased's family, friends, and ministers to help them express their gratitude for the person's life. These tributes included sentiments like "He never met a stranger" and "She laughed every day." Reading the obituaries reminded me that people are often good and that I need to make my days count.

The obituaries in the *New York Times* are different from the ones in the *Paoli News-Republican*. The people in Paoli would balk at paying $263 for the first four lines and $52 per line thereafter with twenty-eight characters per line. Most of the people in my old church would not be able to read the seven-point sans-serif font without a magnifying glass.

But it is Lent, so I sit down with my new hometown newspaper to look for what matters in the obituaries. Here is some of what I have found:

- Lerone Bennett, Jr., 89, wrote *Before the Mayflower* in which he noted that the first blacks arrived in the colonies in 1619. He worked to prepare students to live in a multi-racial society.
- Allayne Berkrot, 88, was a dedicated elementary school teacher who loved children. She was a vivacious, passionate, and caring person.
- Peggy Cafritz, 70, was a civil rights activist, arts patron, and educator. She practiced a radical kind of love, fostering and mentoring countless young people, including one former gang member who needed $8,000 to pay her college tuition.

- Mary Dwyer, 94, fought a determined battle against bipolar disorder. While she was never able to conquer it, she never let it conquer her.
- Marilyn Henry, 89, was one of the first females to graduate from Chicago Medical School. During the 1960s she marched and sang on the front lines of the civil rights movement.
- George Kaufmann, 89, loved the closing lines of a song by his dear friend, Tony Bennett: "'Cause I must be leaving, it was fun. Now it's done. So long, big time. I gotta run."
- Elizabeth Landauer, 80, served as a Girl Scout leader for many years.
- Ruth Meyers, 95, was a chemist who founded Women Strike for Peace.
- Marjorie Neikrug-Rasking, 103, passed away begrudgingly and peacefully. She was pre-deceased by five husbands.
- Patricia Rashkin, 74, chose a career as a guardian for those unable to fend for themselves, spending more than three decades with the City of New York's protective services.
- Richard Rosenblatt, 91, was the author of *On Borrowed Time*, his memories of encounters with movie stars, moguls, scientists, generals, explorers, athletes, crooks, and sociopaths.
- William Selden, 70, businessman, philanthropist, sportsman, dog-lover, and innate comedian. He was a long-time supporter of the Guide Dog Foundation for the Blind.
- Lilian Simon, 97, expressed herself through dance, collage, photography, antiques, fashion, and food.
- Alan Lewis Stein, 88, founded the not-for-profit affordable housing entity, Bridge Housing. Bridge has participated in the development of more than 17,000 units of housing, providing homes for 42,500 people.
- Gertrude Steinburg, 98, was widowed at 53, so she went back to college. Upon graduation she faced age discrimination in the job market. Undaunted, she got a master's in gerontology and worked for thirty years at NYU's Alzheimer's Disease Center.
- Daniel Sullivan, 90, traveled the world extensively, visiting every continent except Antarctica. His wife, Peggy could not be persuaded to travel there as she preferred Tahiti.
- Constance Sultan, 84, worked for thirty years at Mount Sinai Hospital, where she was the charge nurse in the baby nursery.

Reading the obituaries sounds gloomy, but that has not been my experience. I am happy to be reminded that people are often good. Being encouraged to make my days count feels like preparing for Easter.

Trinity Sunday: It's better than "daylight saving time begins" (June 12, 2019)

Trinity Sunday is June 16, but we can forgive ministers who do not mention it. Trinity Sunday has never really caught on. Not only are Christmas and Easter a hundred times bigger, Epiphany is bigger too. Mother's Day—which is not in the Bible—is far bigger than Trinity Sunday. This year we get to see if Father's Day—which is pretty small—is bigger than Trinity Sunday. For most Protestant (and especially Baptist) churches, Trinity Sunday is less significant than "daylight saving time begins."

The unpopularity of Trinity Sunday has to do with the incomprehensibility of the Trinity. Most of the things we talk about on Sunday still sound fine on Monday—kindness, sharing, listening—but others only sound right in church:

"Glory be to the Father, and to the Son, and to the Holy Ghost."

"I baptize you in the name of the Father, Son, and Spirit."

"Holy, Holy, Holy, Lord God Almighty, God in three persons, blessed Trinity."

We sing, confess our faith, and baptize with Trinitarian formulas, but you seldom hear someone in line at Starbucks say, "How 'bout that God in three persons?"

The Trinity is confusing. It is usually Father, Son, and Holy Ghost, but sometimes you hear Creator, Redeemer, and Sustainer, or Almighty God, Incarnate Word, and Holy Comforter. What about this one: Womb of Life, Word in Flesh, and Brooding Spirit? This could be your new favorite: Primordial Nature, Consequent Nature, and Superjective Nature.

We sing "God in three persons," but one theologian suggests it would be more accurate to sing "God in three hypostatic modes of being." That is not going to catch on.

The Bible does not contain the word "Trinity." Not until the fourth century did church leaders formalize the idea at the Council of Nicea. Different theologians express it in different ways.

John Calvin writes, "To the Father is attributed the beginning of activity and the fountain and wellspring of all things; to the Son, wisdom, counsel, and the ordered disposition of all things; but to the Spirit is assigned the power and efficacy of that activity." Too bad that won't fit on a bumper sticker.

Karl Barth explains, "God is the speaker, without whom there is no word and no meaning, the word who is the speaker's word and the bearer of the meaning, the meaning which is as much the meaning of the speaker as of the word." Glad he cleared that up.

For most of us, the hairsplitting intellectual gymnastics of arguments concerning essence versus substance seem obscure. The analogies are inadequate but clever. Father, Son, and Spirit are like water in the form of liquid, ice, and steam. They are like the sun, the rays of the sun, and the heat generated by the sun. They are like the memory, understanding, and love that exist in the same heart.

My junior high Sunday school teacher's favorite was that Jesus is the pitcher, the Spirit is the catcher, and the Father is the umpire. (No one ever confused my teacher with Karl Barth.)

Ultimately, the Trinity is impossible to explain. It seems like such an esoteric discussion that we are tempted to think it doesn't matter, but it does.

We spend most of our lives dealing with questions that are easy to answer. What's for lunch? Who won the game? How much money do I have? Such questions pass the time, but now and then we realize that staying on the surface keeps us from the good gifts that are deeper down.

The doctrine of the Trinity reminds us that there is more to God than we can sing or preach or prove. God is as near as our breath, but not so familiar as to be completely understood. God is beyond time and space, but not so mysterious as to be inaccessible.

The Trinity is the understanding that God is at work in an abundance of ways. God is in the world, the story of Christ, and the peace deep within us. God draws us to abundant life through the wonder of creation, the love of Jesus, and the hope that holds us. God is over us as Creator, with us as Christ, and in us as Spirit.

The Trinity offers direction on how we should live. If we believe that God created all the world, then our attitude will be celebration and concern. If we believe that God was in Christ, then we will follow Jesus' example of caring. If we believe that the Spirit is present, then we will look for the ways God is at work.

Explaining the Trinity is like describing the ocean to someone who has never seen more than a teaspoon of water, but Trinity Sunday might be a good Sunday to give your dad a tie—and to enjoy a difficult, delightful truth.

Reformation Day—498 years and counting (October 30, 2015)

Seminary professors spend a lot of time around twenty-four-year-olds. As a result, we spend a lot of time feeling old. Our church experience is different from theirs.

My parents took me to church three times a week. My students' mothers took them to church when they did not have soccer practice.

I competed in Bible drills. My students walk labyrinths.

My Bible is on the nightstand, next to my glasses. Their Bible is on their phone.

We had a water fountain in the hall. They have coffee bars in the sanctuary.

They were taught that the church exists to care for God's children. My church's goal was to be bigger than the Methodist church.

I was baptized during a Sunday night service with ten other eight-year-olds. Some of my students were baptized on Saturday night in a swimming pool. They have the selfies to prove it.

Some of my students are in churches that have established Twitter hashtags to encourage people to share sermon quotes. I do not know what that means.

Most Baptist churches have lots of people my age. My students tell me that when they visit some churches, they receive the kind of welcome a unicorn or some other mythical creature might receive.

According to the Barna Research Group, 59 percent of young Christians disconnect from church life after the age of fifteen for at least a year. Churches work best for those whose career paths are conventional—leave home, get an education, find a job, get married, and have kids—all before the age of thirty. Churches are not as good at the new normal—putting that stuff off as long as you can.

These young adults do not wander away from church for any one reason. They have a list of complaints. They complain that churches focus more on the institution than on God. They think that churches are not diverse. They believe churches are anti-science, and they do not want to choose between their pastor and biology professor. They struggle with what chastity means when they are getting married much later. They feel like churches are hostile to LGBTQs. They want to be accepting and say they do not find that acceptance in the church. They want to know why the church is not what it should be, why the church is such a bureaucracy, and why the church is not more like Jesus. Some twentysomethings lower their expectations, some stay irritated, and many walk away, but the best do not give up or give in. They help us become a better church.

Martin Luther was thirty-three when he posted his famous list of complaints. Luther was angry about the immorality of the priests and their irreverence for holy things. He was so disillusioned with the church that he became a theology professor. Teaching the Bible led him away from his experience in the church to the grace of God. He came to love the

God he used to fear. He discovered that God accepts sinful people. Luther complained because the church had not taught him that acceptance.

On All Hallows' Eve, October 31, 1517, Luther nailed ninety-five theses to the church door in Wittenberg. Others agreed that the church should be given to faith rather than fear. The church changed because Martin Luther believed it could be better and complained.

The church can still be better. The comfortable approach to faith is as popular now as when Luther challenged it. Churches are less likely to declare like Luther, "Here I stand!" than to ask like a marketer, "What do people want?"

Serving each other is simpler than serving those who most need help. Talking about prayer is less difficult than giving up security and comfort. Studying the Bible is easier than hearing Christ's challenge.

Yet God is still at work. God is making the church more open, compassionate, and bold. The Spirit draws us to give ourselves in worship, care for one another, and grow in grace. The Spirit pushes us to minister to those with the greatest needs. The Spirit helps us hear Scripture calling us to become more like Jesus.

Many who have been in church all their lives are amazed at the new ways congregations are living as God's people. Churches have discovered that Christianity is not something you study but something you do. Churches are tutoring underprivileged children, caring for senior citizens, and sharing meals with the hungry. Some of the ways churches are acting like Christ were not happening twenty years ago. God is teaching us that the primary issue is not whether the church is getting bigger but whether the church is living like Jesus. Every day is Reformation Day.

Mixed dating and ill-fated love (May 16, 2014)

"Mixed dating."

That phrase is about the only thing I remember our minister of youth saying. Tommy said it after the bell rang to signal the end of Sunday school. None of us wanted to admit that we did not know what mixed dating is, so we hurried off to big church. We were seated in our pew in the back before my friend Meatball had the courage to ask, "What the heck is mixed dating?"

"I think it's double dating."

"No, it's dating someone two years younger than you."

"If he's talking about dating black people, my dad is not going to be happy." (Mississippi, 1974.)

That night we felt more anticipation than usual as Tommy began to speak: "I want to tell you about an error in judgment I made because I don't want you to make the same mistake. I saw her the first day of senior English. She was wearing a blue shirt with white crisscrossed strings down the side. I fell in love, but I didn't ask Donna out on a date until October. We went to see *The Jungle Book*, but I wasn't paying attention to the message—that the jungle boy needed to be with his own kind.

"Like Mowgli, Donna and I didn't talk about the elephant in the room. For six months we did everything together, except for the most important thing. We didn't go to the same church. You see, Donna was a Methodist, so we ended up with broken hearts. Don't date someone you can't marry. Don't get on the train if you can't go to Baltimore."

I thought about Donna and Tommy's ill-fated love when I read about the "One in Christ" Prayer Focus. Southern Baptist leaders are urging their churches to unite through prayer between June 15 (since Father's Day suggests "One Father") and June 21. The hope is "to lead Southern Baptists from diverse backgrounds to unite under the lordship of Jesus" and "remind Southern Baptists to focus on what unites them—Jesus" (*SBC Life*, Pre-convention Special Issue 2014, page 8).

Focusing on Jesus is a fine idea, but pushing for unity among Southern Baptists on the far right and Southern Baptists on the far-flung right is setting the bar too low. Donna should not be off limits anymore.

Any Baptist arguing for unity has the credibility of Donald Sterling speaking on equality. For most of our 400 years, Baptist contributions to the ecumenical movement would fit in a thimble and still rattle around like a BB in a boxcar. Baptists cannot get along with each other, much less with other Christians.

The church has divided and subdivided. If you can still find a copy of the Yellow Pages, let your fingers stroll through the church section. Greater Atlanta claims eighty-five denominations, including Full Gospel (not a compliment to the rest of us) and United Church of Christ (as if there is such a thing).

John Calvin thundered, "There cannot be two or three churches unless Christ is torn asunder," and then started his own denomination. The "one body" has been dismembered with arms and legs strewn all around.

We hope God smiles over our differences because the dark side of our divisions is that we have learned to measure other groups by how close they are to our group. We find it easy to define orthodoxy as our doxy and heresy as everyone else's ideas. We get used to our songs, traditions, and provincialism. We tend to think of ourselves as a team competing against other teams. We buy into the American idea that competition is good for everyone—"free enterprise religion."

Father Joseph and I were competing over which of our two churches is more welcoming: "Joe, if I came to your church, you wouldn't let me take Communion."

If we were playing chess, I would have said, "Check."

Father Joe countered, "If, after a lifetime as a Christian minister, I went to a Baptist church, most of them would insist I be baptized again."

"Checkmate."

I should stop having mixed feelings when one of my seminary's graduates gets a job with the Methodists. We should recognize others' baptisms and ordinations. We should realize that our Baptist distinctives are not as distinct as we were taught. (Most Protestants claim the priesthood of the believers.)

We should be committed to important truths, but the boundaries, whatever boundaries there are, belong to God. Someone should have said that to Tommy and Donna. They would have loved Baltimore.

Jesus loves hippie churches (September 4, 2015)

The parking lot has several versions of "Coexist" and "God loves the whole world no exceptions" bumper stickers, a "Leslie Knope for President," and, on the same Prius, an "I'm too poor to vote Republican." The sign on the sanctuary door says, "Leave your cell phone at home." More recycling bins line the wall than there are types of recycling.

Sixty gentle people gather in another church's building on Sunday afternoon. They could be dressed for a picnic—hiking sandals, Buddy Holly glasses, turquoise jewelry, and wooden cross necklaces. The congregation includes men with gray ponytails, a few Mennonites, a Jewish guy, a philosophy professor, three potters, and the carver who made the Communion plates.

The chairs are in a circle. Banners cover the walls. Candles, at least one of which is amber vanilla, sit on the unused piano. Three guitars lean against the organ that has been pushed to the side. They had a canvas labyrinth for a while, but then they had to return it to the Episcopalians.

As worshipers enter, they are given prayer stones, which were regular stones an hour ago.

The chiming of the hour is on a dulcimer. The music is James Taylor; Peter, Paul, and Mary; and Mumford and Sons before they went electric. Sometimes they sing a stanza in Spanish with bad accents. When the hymn is "Softly and Tenderly," they change "O Sinner" to "Beloved"—which does not quite work.

The prayers of the people take twenty minutes because someone has an epic poem to share. They pray not just for cousins with back trouble but also for those on death row, the hungry, and victims of war. They pray for the city council meeting where the church's political action committee will be arguing that homeless people should be allowed to have campfires during the winter. The congregation takes the chaos of the world so seriously that the worship includes silence. When a child dies, words are insufficient.

Several women knit throughout the sermon, which is a call to live against the grain. Christians are to "tell the truth in a world that lies, give in a world that takes, make peace in a world that fights, care for the environment in a world that feels little concern for creation, and carry a cross in a world that crucifies those who love."

The children take the gluten-free body of Christ first. There are two options for the blood of Jesus: one non-alcoholic and one real wine.

They pass the peace with gusto. "The peace of Christ be with you" sounds like "I love seeing your face."

When the primary worship traditions in the United States are named, the list usually consists of "Liturgical, Evangelical, Pentecostal, and Contemporary." Some of Jesus' favorites are overlooked. If the Yellow Pages still exist, they still do not have a category for "Churches—Hippie," but they should.

The Gospels make it clear that Jesus loves hippie churches. Jesus walks everywhere. He travels with a band of troubadours. He hikes in the mountains. He talks to God.

Jesus does not work in an office. He spends time with social outcasts. He has strong words about hypocrites. He criticizes the establishment.

Jesus loves birds and flowers. He says that peacemakers are the children of God. He would fit right in at a drum circle.

In the Sermon on the Mount, Jesus sounds like the preacher at a hippie church: "If you decide to live for God, you won't need a steak on the table or care whether the collar on your shirt is frayed. You won't get caught up in trivialities like diamond rings. Blue jeans are plenty comfortable. Look at the birds, free and unfettered, singing their songs, carefree in the love of God. They don't worry about climbing the corporate ladder and yet God cares for them. No matter how many nips and tucks you get or how often you have your hair highlighted, you're wasting every minute you spend in front of the mirror. Instead of walking through Saks Fifth Avenue and looking for what's in fashion, walk through the fields and look at the scarlet poppies. They never primp, but have you ever seen colors so beautiful?

Bradley Cooper looks like a Baptist minister when compared with wild-flowers. If God gives attention to flowers—most of which are never even seen—don't you think God will care for you?"

Jesus loves congregations filled with peaceful souls who are willing to walk out of step from the crowd. We need more hippie churches because most of us are too at ease in the world. We are not nearly uncomfortable enough with the way things are.

Snake charmers (August 16, 2013)

If you've been searching for a new favorite show on television since Matthew Crawley, heir of Lord Grantham, died on *Downton Abbey*, then mark September 10 on your calendar. That is when *Snake Salvation* debuts on the National Geographic Channel.

This much-anticipated reality show follows a pair of serpent-handling Pentecostal preachers, Andrew Hamblin of Tabernacle Church of God in La Follette, Tennessee, and Jamie Coots of Full Gospel Tabernacle in Jesus Name Church of Middlesboro, Kentucky.

The Reverends Hamblin and Coots take with dead seriousness a specific portion of Mark 16:17-18: "These signs shall follow them that believe; in my name shall they cast out devils; they shall speak with new tongues; they shall take up serpents; and if they drink any deadly thing, it shall not hurt them."

Some disapprove—serpent handling is illegal in narrow-minded states like Tennessee and Kentucky—but Holiness churchgoers have been "dancing with the snakes" for over 100 years.

The show will feature worshipers petting venomous reptiles in church and living within a broad definition of "normal" outside of church. The series hopes to make it clear that churchgoers who wrestle rattlers have the same everyday struggles with marriage, money, and moccasins as the rest of us.

Only sixteen programs have been planned, but this show is here to stay. Look for these upcoming episodes: "Bitten in Church," "Sin or Serpents," and "Outlaw Religion."

I am hoping the second season will include "New Testament Scholar" in which a seminary professor (a snake in the grass?) explains that Mark 16:9-20 is a later addition to the text. I would set my DVR for an episode titled "But What If This Passage Is a Metaphor?" I would be less enthused about a "Downing Drano" episode in which church members test the "drink any deadly thing" portion of the text.

Snake Salvation could begin a flood of church-based reality shows as television producers begin to realize the dramatic possibilities of combining the allure of reality TV with the reality of church life. Here are a few possibilities:

America's Next Top Middle School Sunday School Teacher. Eighth graders try the patience of well-meaning but naïve educators who are not sure how to respond to "Where in the Bible does it say that God thinks polygamy is a bad idea?"

The Bachelor. Ten hopelessly romantic women compete for the hand of one tall, handsome, Bible-believing man. Follow the struggles of the most attractive male in the singles' group as he weighs the appeal of women who may be at church at 9:45 on Sunday morning for reasons other than their love for Jesus.

Deacon Dynasty. This cast of old and powerful church leaders brings drama to a new level. Their heated conversations will keep you wondering what these bad boys and girls will say next. Watch them struggle to escape an old paradigm.

Heaven's Kitchen. Aspiring chefs are put to the ultimate challenge of competing for recognition as the church's best cook. Cutthroat casseroles!

The Real Housewives of the Church. This drama details the cast's lives, loves, and religious concerns. Churchgoing housewives in Orange County, Miami, and Beverly Hills are more interesting than housewives who have never wondered how their hairstyle goes with their choir robe.

Trading Musicians. Each Sunday, churches with radically different worship styles trade musicians with hilarious results. Watch the senior adults' faces when the first note of the prelude is played on an electric guitar.

Survivor. Members of a ministers' peer group meet each month in an undisclosed location and choose one pastor to go into the insurance business.

And my favorite suggestion: *Church in the Real World.* Shows like *Snake Salvation* suggest that, for a few, church is an escape from reality, but the opposite is more often true. The world of popular culture is not as real as the hope of Christ's often dramatic church.

I am part of the resistance inside the American church (September 7, 2018)

The church is facing a test unlike any faced in the modern era. It is not just that the church is bitterly divided over politics. The dilemma is that not nearly enough of the church's leadership is working diligently from within to frustrate the church's worst inclinations.

I would know. I am one of them.

To be clear, ours is not the popular "resistance" of those who are leaving the church. We want the church to succeed and think that in many ways the church has shared the love of God. But we believe our first duty is to God, and the church continues to act in a manner that is detrimental to the health of God's people. That is why many ministers have vowed to do what we can to preserve the church from the church's more misguided impulses.

The root of the problem is the church's lack of love. Anyone who works in the church knows the church is not always moored to the discernible first principle that should guide decision making. Although the church is meant to be Christ to the world, the church has often shown little affinity for the ideals espoused by Christ—feeding the hungry, welcoming immigrants, loving your enemies, praying with humility, and caring for the poor.

At best, the church has invoked these ideals in scripted settings. At worst, the church has attacked them outright.

In addition to the mass-marketing of the notion that God's world is the "enemy of the church," the impulses are generally anti-love.

Don't get me wrong. There are bright spots that the near-ceaseless negative coverage of the church fails to capture: openness to faith, acts of kindness, and concern for the hurting. But these successes have come despite—not because of—most of the church's leadership, which is often adversarial, petty, and ineffective.

From the pulpit to the pew, churchgoers will privately admit their disbelief at the ways the church focuses on buildings, bylaws, and budgets to the neglect of those the church is meant to serve. Many are working to insulate their spirituality from the narrowness of much of the church.

Church meetings veer off the topic of God's love, get consumed by repetitive complaints, and end up with policy discussions that have little to do with sharing hope.

A church member complained to me recently, exasperated by a church meeting, "There was no mention of God after the opening prayer."

The erratic behavior of the church would be more concerning if it were not for unsung heroes in the church. Some of these people seem unimportant, but they go to great lengths to keep bad decisions contained in the institution of the church, though they are clearly not always successful.

It may be cold comfort in this chaotic era, but Americans should know that there are followers of Christ in the church. We fully recognize what is happening. And we are trying to do what's right even when the church won't.

The result is a two-track church.

Take foreign policy: In public and in private, much of the church shows a preference for an autocratic president and displays little genuine appreciation for the ties that bind us all as children of God. Astute observers have noted, though, that much of the church is operating on another track, one where God's love is the guiding principle and where broken people are engaged as peers rather than ridiculed as rivals.

This is not the work of the deep church. It is the work of the real church.

Given the inauthenticity they have witnessed, many have left the church. But many others have stayed to steer the church in the right direction until—one way or another—it's over.

The bigger concern is not what church leadership has done to the church but rather what we as church members have allowed them to do to us. We have sunk low with them and allowed our discourse to be stripped of civility.

The church can, as Senator John McCain put it in his farewell letter, "break free of the tribalism trap," with the high aim of uniting through our shared values and love of God.

There is a quiet resistance within the church of people choosing to put God first. But the real difference will be made by everyday church members rising above politics, reaching across the aisle, and resolving to shed the labels in favor of a single one: God's people.

Editor's Note: This op-ed is wholly dependent on "I Am Part of the Resistance inside the Trump Administration," published anonymously on September 5, 2018, by the *New York Times.*

How churches that don't think they are anti-Semitic promote anti-Semitism (August 16, 2019)

The shooter in the synagogue in Poway, California, in April turned out to be a member of an Orthodox Presbyterian Church. The church released this statement: "We are wounded to the core that such an evil could have gone out from our community. Such hatred has no place in any part of our beliefs and practices, for we seek to shape our whole lives according to the love and gospel of Jesus Christ."

"Wounded to the core" is a good start, but where is the word of repentance? Where is the self-examination that leads to change and different outcomes? Churches do not often think about how they encourage anti-Semitism.

Harassment of Jews is increasing worldwide. The United Kingdom has recorded its highest number of anti-Semitic attacks in each of the last three years. In the United States more than half of religious hate crimes are aimed at Jews, even though Jews represent less than two percent of the population.

Historically, the church has contributed a particularly ugly strain of anti-Semitism. In the twelfth century, Christians came up with the horrible idea of blood libel. This lie was that Jews murdered Christian children to use their blood for ritual purposes. On as many as 100 occasions Christians massacred Jews in response to the disappearance of a child.

Martin Luther, who may be the most important figure in the last five hundred years of Christian history, was anti-Semitic. He wrote a treatise, *The Jews and Their Lies*, which includes the line, "we are at fault in not slaying them." Historians tend to say that Luther was great except for his anti-Semitism—which is embarrassing for the historians. You cannot be great and anti-Semitic.

A line can be drawn from Luther's influence to the Holocaust. Centuries of Christian anti-Semitism made Hitler possible. In 1936, the Baptist World Alliance met in Berlin under the banner of the swastika and received greetings from Hitler. Baptists returned to the United States to report on the wonderful things happening in Germany.

The Catholic Church played a role in the rise of Nazism. John Cornwell's biography of Pius XII was titled *Hitler's Pope*.

The church has not just been on the wrong side of history, but on the wrong side of Christianity.

Most churches in America today do not think they are anti-Semitic. But many churches allow small attacks on Judaism that make larger attacks more likely. Churches should ask, "Would an anti-Semitic person be uncomfortable in our congregation?" because every person in the church should know that anti-Semitism is antithetical to Christianity.

The names "Old Testament" and "New Testament" are themselves unfair, but some Christian preachers suggest the God of the Old Testament is different from the God of the New Testament, that the Old Testament God is angry while the New Testament God is merciful. This is not true to Judaism or Christianity.

Christians often fail to recognize that the Gospels describe arguments within Judaism and not arguments between Judaism and Christianity (which did not yet exist). Jesus is often set in opposition to first-century Judaism as though Jesus was the only one who valued women or worked for the oppressed. Jesus learned to value women and care for the poor from his

Jewish context. When Jesus said, "Love God" and "Love your neighbor," he was quoting the Hebrew Scriptures.

Putting down Judaism to make Jesus look good makes no sense.

Christians need to see what is at stake. Anti-Semitism is by definition a repudiation of Christianity as well as of Judaism, and an enemy of pluralism and democracy. Religious intolerance breeds greater intolerance.

A Christian youth minister takes her middle schoolers to a service at a Jewish synagogue. Afterwards a 14-year-old says, "They do what we do. They sing. They read the Bible. They pray. They stole our stuff."

Churches can start with the simple step of remembering that Jesus was Jewish. Christians should encourage an appreciation for Judaism, because the best Christian values are Jewish.

On most Sundays a few Jewish people worship with our congregation in Brooklyn. You might think that would not change anything, but it does. I show a greater respect for our Jewish heritage, quote more Jewish scholars and speak out more often on incidents of anti-Semitism. I have learned that I need to preach as though there are always Jewish people present. Congregations need to listen as though there are always Jewish people present.

Last month I preached at a synagogue on Friday and the rabbi preached at our church on Sunday. We did this because we need to learn more about and from each other.

I need this to be more Christian.

Worship Notes

Two Days with the Monks: Protestant Envy, Confusion, and Gratitude (January 16, 2020)

Benedictine monks pride themselves on hospitality, take vows of silence, and see no tension between these two. On the first morning of my retreat, a construction worker gave me directions to the dining hall and added a strangely sarcastic, "Enjoy!"

At breakfast, guests are expected to stand behind their chairs until the monks have been served. This practice is difficult to communicate without speaking.

I took more food than anyone else—a piece of toast, a black banana, and a bowl of indistinguishable cereal. Eating at a crowded table without speaking can be creepy. We tend to avoid eye contact when we are not talking, so we stared at our food. I sneezed and felt guilty. No one said, "God bless you."

I confess that I skipped Matins, the 6:00 a.m. service, but I made it to Mass, Sext, Vespers, and Compline—services that take place when normal people are awake. I found praying the hours confusing. Working out of one worship book would have been helpful. The ribbons were not in the right places in *Monastic Antiphonary*. I would have gladly paid extra for an order of worship.

Following the monk next to you is not as easy as you might think. They have the order memorized. The passing of the peace was a few unenthusiastic nods. Chanting can get old. I have mixed feelings about kissing the Bible.

I tried not to stick out, but I failed. I still don't know the Nicene Creed. They changed one of the lines that Protestants knew. The response to "The Lord be with you," which I knew as "and also with you," is now "and with your Spirit." They clearly changed this response to confuse Protestants. I mistakenly said the last verse of the Lord's Prayer—the one every Catholic knows does not belong. During confession I forgot to thump my chest at "through my fault." If there had been a genuflecting class, I would have flunked. At one point the monk next to me scratched his head, so I scratched mine.

Whenever I cracked the code I was delighted. I learned that at the Gospel reading, monks sign the cross on their foreheads, mouths, and chests to ask God to be present in their minds, lips, and hearts.

I tried to do what the monks did, but I was *acting* like a monk. They *are* monks. Since the sixth century Benedictines have promised to "Prefer nothing to the love of Christ." Monks do not care much about how they look, though their black robes are stylish—especially the hoods. I envy the way they sprinkle water as a reminder of our baptisms, swing incense as a call to prayer, and wear hats in worship—though maybe not a miter.

I do not often kneel when I pray, but it would lead me to a greater sense of humility. I do not keep a crucifix in every room, but it would help me think about God's suffering. I do not cross myself a dozen times a day, but I need ways to remember God's presence.

The monks are following Christ and ignoring culture. We need to admire those who live with a different understanding of success. I am jealous of their simplicity though I am not yet ready to get rid of my stuff.

My last meal with the brothers was lunch, the one time we were allowed to talk. The monks complained about monasteries that don't take silence seriously enough and allow conversation at two meals a day: "C'mon man, it's a monastery!"

The Benedictines poked fun at other orders: "You know how those Dominicans are."

A parish priest, who was also a guest, said, "I don't want to go back to my church. The silence here is so wonderful and my congregation is so noisy."

Silence is a gift, but so is a noisy congregation. Two days in a monastery is a gift, but so is realizing that you belong somewhere else.

Churches, wake up and smell the coffee: Communion with a cup of joe? (August 28, 2018)

"Should we say something to her?"

"It's not her fault. She didn't grow up in church."

The object of concern brought a cup of coffee into the sanctuary and set it down on the pew. The troubled church members tried to let her know telepathically that coffee is not allowed in the sanctuary. How could she miss the invisible line beyond which a cup of joe is not permitted?

But how could the church not see that in a world that is asleep, coffee is NoDoz?

Coffee appears only two times in *The Message* Bible: "Never again will friends drop in for coffee" (Job 7:10) and "Wait table for me until I've finished my coffee" (Luke 17:8). Imagine how many times "coffee" would be in the concordance if Jesus had thought to change water into cappuccinos at the wedding in Cana.

Opening the church to coffee drinkers has been a long, difficult struggle. Coffee dates back to the 15th century and the Sufi monasteries of Yemen. One legend is that the mystic Ghothul Akbar Nooruddin Abu al-Hasan al-Shadhili was traveling in Ethiopia. He saw birds acting unusually lively, and upon trying the berries that the birds had been eating, experienced the same vitality. Coffee was soon part of religious practice in the Islamic world. The Sufis used the beverage to keep themselves alert during nighttime devotions and as a kind of spiritual intoxication when they chanted the name of God.

Because Muslims loved coffee, several Christian groups, including the Ethiopian Orthodox Church, made a big brouhaha and banned coffee. Mormons still avoid this potion made with magic beans.

Churches need to wake up and smell the coffee. When I ask Siri to "find coffee" she lists four places within 800 feet of my house. Our neighborhood has more coffee shops than churches.

Coffee is the most important meal of the day for many. In the midst of the daily grind, coffee is invigorating. A yawn is a silent scream for coffee. Sleep is a symptom of caffeine deprivation. Coffee smells like freshly ground heaven and tastes like hopes and dreams.

When we hold a cup of coffee, the warmth radiates through our hands. The aroma drifts through the air. The cream magically changes coffee from black to good-to-the-last-drop caramel. This sensual experience helps our sleepy selves greet the day with gratitude as we reflect on what we now have the energy to achieve.

Worship would be less lively without a cup of joe. We can tell a lot about a church from how it caffeinates its worshipers. My parents' Baptist church is Folgers. Unitarians drink fair trade coffee. Mennonites have Keurig committees that wash and recycle those little cups. Presbyterians fill their fellowship halls for the sacrament of coffee hour. Catholics serve decaf at midnight mass. Sharing coffee is a way of saying, "We love you a latte."

Church should be a place for common ground and a home to hang your mug. "Bible study" is less enticing than "Coffee and Bible study." Nominating committees should choose a church barista.

"Would you like a cup of coffee?" is an offer of friendship. Coffee turns a counseling session into a conversation between friends. Saying "yes" to coffee at the end of a meal is a promise to hang around.

Here is a question that needs to percolate: would coffee be a better symbol for communion? Grape juice is dull. Wine puts you to sleep. Coffee refreshes, revives and stimulates. The Lord's Table could be a coffee table. If we drank coffee at communion, we could get rid of those tiny shot glasses. Picture the communion cup holders on the backs of pews becoming real cup holders. Coffee would be a fine symbol for the enlivening of the Spirit that happens at the table.

We should take our coffee seriously and joyfully. We should fill our churches with sugar and cream, sweetness and light.

Too busy to sing? Try anyway (September 29, 2016)

I go to work on Tuesday with a detailed to-do list. If everything goes perfectly, I will end the day writing a column. If I get through six of the ten items, it will be a productive day. If I get through five, I will have kept up. If I only get through four, I will be seriously behind.

I get off to a good start but make the mistake of checking email. (Don't look at your email if you want to get things done.) I have seven messages to which I need to respond. The wonderful sermon ideas I had on Monday are now clearly unacceptable. I remember something I was supposed to have done a week ago.

Someone I want to talk to drops by. I have several conversations with children at Plymouth Church School. Carol is having lunch with a friend, so I am on my own for lunch—which I should have realized before I went home at noon.

On Tuesday afternoon, we have worship planning and staff meetings. I enjoy both, even when they go long. At 6, I have checked off three of the ten items on my to-do list.

I want to keep working, but I have told choir members that I will go to the Hymn Sing at 7. I do not have time to sing, but I take my bad attitude with me to the choir room.

Our minister of music, Bruce Oelschlager—whose name makes me think of German beer—has chosen international hymns. We start with a Spanish tune, "Come Christians, Join to Sing."

The people in attendance are smart enough to know that if we do not want to sing, then we have lost our way. Music is yoga for people who do not want to wear yoga pants.

We sing a Brazilian hymn, "O Sing to the Lord/Cantad al Senor"— which is Spanish though Brazilians speak Portuguese. I consider raising my hand to complain.

We sing a Scottish song with the wonderful line, "The house of faith has many rooms where we have never been."

People who sing are happier than people who do not. Singing makes it hard to stay frustrated.

We sing "Christ beside Me," a Gaelic hymn based on the Prayer of St. Patrick from the fifth century.

I am no longer thinking about what I should have gotten done.

We sing the Ghanaian hymn "Jesu, Jesu" and ask God to "fill us with your love."

Singing reminds us of things that are not on our to-do lists.

Martin Luther wrote, "Music is a lovely gift of God which has often wakened and moved me. Music drives away the devil and makes people forget all wrath, unchastity, arrogance, and the like. My heart bubbles up and overflows in response to music, which has so often refreshed me and delivered me from dire plagues."

When the world seems bent on madness, music offers hope.

Imagine you get to the symphony just as the orchestra begins to warm up and sit down next to a well-dressed gentleman. You introduce yourself and ask what he does. He responds, "I'm a musician, a conductor."

You say, "I don't want to take advantage of you, but I've never been able to figure out what's going on during warm-ups."

He begins pointing things out: "That violinist is practicing the overture. That cellist is putting her music in order, studying the score. The bassist is staring at the hardest part. The percussionist is playing the same notes over and over because he only has eight measures to play all night."

The orchestra begins to tune their instruments. Every instrument is silent, then the oboe plays a note. Everyone plays a note. The oboe plays a note. The conductor explains that the oboe cannot be tuned to anything else, so the other instruments tune to the oboe. You start listening for the oboe. You are listening more intently and hearing more.

If we listen carefully, we can hear the music of God's love and tune our lives to it. When we are too busy to sing, we should sing. If we are too tired to sing, we should try. If we think we are too important to sing, we need to sing.

Skipping Christmas (December 22, 2011)

For centuries, Christians have celebrated the birth of Jesus by coming to church to sing, pray, remember, give thanks, and recommit our lives to Christ. What were we thinking?

This year, with Christmas falling on Sunday, many churches have decided that the best way to celebrate the coming of Christ is to cancel worship. The primary reason given is that attendance will be sparse. When did we decide that the purpose of worship is to draw a crowd? Attendance at the first Christmas was not big, but God decided to go ahead with it anyway.

Another reason offered is that canceling worship is in keeping with a "family-friendly" approach. Pastor Aaron Orlinski of Grace Church in Melbourne, Florida, says, "Christmas is a big family day, and we're focused on the family. We should be able to worship the Lord in our homes, also."

Huh? Does this mean churches should encourage members to gather with their family for brunch on Easter or go bowling together on Good Friday? When did we get the idea that the primary purpose of the church is to support the family? The New Testament teaches that the church is our family. Christians put Christ ahead of their family. Jesus felt this so strongly that he said, "Whoever comes to me and does not hate father and mother, wife and children, brothers and sisters cannot be my disciple." (This verse is not going to make it on to anybody's Christmas card.)

What about the people without a family at home—the elderly, the isolated, the lonely, those a long distance from family? Isn't it possible that some of those who are alone at Christmas also need to worship God?

The big issue is not that people will skip church on Sunday. The real problem is that churches are failing to tell the truth about Christmas. It is hard to read the Gospels and see how our modern Christmas celebrations could have begun with the ancient story of the first Christmas. In the Bible, Christmas is not about big crowds, family gatherings or expensive presents.

The first Christmas marks the beginning of a small, counter-cultural community of people who put their trust in God's way and none of their faith in materialism and selfishness. Christmas invites us to have different standards, hopes, and dreams from those who do not know the meaning of Christ's coming.

If we believe that Jesus' birth changes the world, then we will change the way we see our world. The work of Christ's hands will be continued in the work of our hands. We will have compassion for all people—especially those who are usually left out. Because Jesus has come, we will walk out of step with the rhythms of the world.

On Sunday, Christians would do well to gather, sing, pray, and listen to the story. We should celebrate by remembering the first Christmas and giving ourselves again to the one born in Bethlehem.

Let's keep Herod in Christmas (December 26, 2014)

Twenty-eight Christmases ago, when I was the new pastor of Central Baptist Church in Paoli, Indiana, I decided to have the church's first Christmas Eve candlelight communion service. I wanted everything to be perfect.

Snow fell that afternoon. A high school junior, Melody Lawson, played "What Child Is This?" on the flute. Three generations—a grandmother, her daughter, and granddaughter—lit the Advent candles. We sang the carols—"O Come, All Ye Faithful," "Away in a Manger," and "O Little Town of Bethlehem." We read the story—Mary, Joseph, the baby, and the manger. I thought, "This is a Hallmark card of a worship service. This is as picture-perfect a Christmas moment as any church has ever known."

That's when Danny Hickman's beeper went off. Danny was a member of the volunteer fire department. When his beeper sounded, as it often did—and it was ten times more likely to go off in church than anywhere else—Danny ran out of the sanctuary. We had almost gotten used to it, but it was disconcerting.

We started singing "Silent Night." Just as we got to "Wondrous Star, lend thy light," Danny ran back in and shouted that Bob Lawson's mother's house was on fire. Bob, his wife, Linda, and their daughter Melody ran out after Danny. Danny's wife got up and left. Everyone had to choose between listening to the preacher's sermon or slipping out one by one and going to a big fire.

By the time I got Mary and Joseph to Bethlehem, the crowd—and I use that term loosely—was made up of those who were waiting for a ride home and those who had fallen asleep. That's not how Christmas Eve candlelight communion services are supposed to turn out. Tragedies should wait until January because they do not fit our ideas about Christmas.

That is why the days after Christmas are a good time to think about King Herod. The horrifying sequence of events in Matthew's Gospel does not feel like it belongs in the Christmas story. The most difficult part to cast in the Christmas pageant is King Herod. Any child who wants to play Herod should not be trusted to play Herod. Walmart sells a variety of plastic nativity scenes for the yard, but there are no glow-in-the-dark King Herods.

No Christmas card has this verse from Matthew on the front: "A voice was heard in Ramah, wailing and loud lamentation." Herod's order called for the death of every male infant in Bethlehem. Matthew cannot find words terrifying enough to describe the horror, so he borrows words from the prophet Jeremiah: "weeping and great mourning, Rachel weeping for her children; she refuses to be consoled because they are no more."

During my second Christmas season as pastor of Central Baptist Church, I got a phone call from the county hospital on December 23. The night before, a teenager had given birth to a stillborn baby. The social worker wanted me to lead a graveside service the next morning. She explained that they would normally have the service a day later or at least in the afternoon, but she "didn't want the girl to associate this experience with Christmas." The teenager had visited our church a few times several months earlier. She was fifteen and had been raped by her grandfather.

Christmas Eve was miserable. The snow had been on the ground for more than a week. It had rained and so the snow was not pretty anymore. The temperature was in the twenties. The sky was dark and threatening to rain again.

Her older sister brought her straight from the hospital. Their parents did not come. They blamed their daughter for the rape. There were six of us there: the teenager, her sister, the funeral director, two women from our church, and me. I knew what I had been told: "We don't want her to associate this experience with Christmas." But I kept thinking about the story that Matthew tells. But I kept thinking about the story that Matthew tells. Christmas is about "wailing and loud lamentation, weeping and great mourning . . . refusing to be consoled, because they are no more" (Matt 2:18).

Christmas is not good news of a great joy that will make everything easy. God comes into the noise and storms, wind and wailing, dying children, raging soldiers, and devastated parents. God shares the pain of everyone whose life is falling apart. The promise of this holy season is that God's hope is deeper than our sadness.

At church with the Carters (October 18, 2013)

At first glance, a supply preacher might turn it down. The church is 183 miles away. The congregation is smaller than most church choirs. The service is on Sunday evening. (I have a prejudice against Sunday night church because I did not see the beginning of *The Wizard of Oz* or the first half of a Super Bowl until I went to college.)

But this Sunday night service was at Jimmy Carter's church. How could I say no when the directions include, "The church is just past the only red light and the giant peanut"?

I did not let my hopes get too high. I kept my imagination under control. This is how I pictured it:

The worship service would be charming. I would preach warmly and thoughtfully.

When the former president shook my hand afterward, he would say, "Brett, I am so glad to get to hear you preach. I read your columns for Associated Baptist Press. The one on Sarah Palin cracked me up.

I hope you don't mind that I brought one of your books for you to sign. Could you make it out to 'Rosalynn and Jimmy, my dear friends'? Would you like to write a book together? You pick the subject.

I have a speech coming up in Israel. Do you want to go? Would your son Caleb be interested in a summer job at the Carter Center? I have a granddaughter who is single whom I would love to have meet Graham. Why don't you spend Christmas with us in Plains? Could we have our picture made with you?"

On the drive to the middle of nowhere, I worked on my opening lines should the former leader of the free world show up:

"Mr. President, you were the first candidate for whom I voted. Too bad it was 1980."

"How about that Congress? What a bunch of goobers!"

"When is the last time you saw Fritz Mondale?"

"I love Willie Nelson, too."

On Sunday night at 6:00, twenty of us gathered in a pecan grove in a modest brick building in the fellowship hall of Maranatha Baptist Church—no suits, no ties, and no president.

God and I had a talk. I apologized for being disappointed that Jimmy and Rosalynn were not there. I told God that I felt terrible for acting like God's presence was somehow not enough to get excited about.

The pianist played, "You may have all this world, just give me Jesus." We sang, "'Tis so sweet to trust in Jesus, just to take him at his word." The announcements included delivering food to the needy, a joint worship service with the Lutherans, and a Gideon speaker.

We prayed to the Creator of the universe for sick friends and gave thanks for a ten-year-old girls' soccer game. We listened to 1 Chronicles 16:11-12, "Seek God's presence continually. Remember the wonderful works God has done."

I preached about the way in which we see God with us now by remembering the way God has been with us in the past. We sang "Surely Goodness and Mercy" and closed with the promise of God's blessing.

What if we only got to worship once every ten years? Wouldn't we tell our children bedtime stories about the last time we went to worship? Wouldn't we mark the date on the calendar in red? Wouldn't we marvel at the possibility of praying together? Wouldn't we wonder at the privilege of singing praises? Wouldn't we write stories and take pictures?

But we get to worship every week. Every Sunday we have the opportunity to worship so it becomes the opportunity to take worship for granted. We miss the miraculous hope of worshiping God.

Brett, Rosalynn, Carol, and Jimmy

The world's most famous Sunday school teacher, his lovely wife, and their Secret Service agents arrived at 6:05.

After the worship service, Rosalynn asked Carol about our children. We compared notes on growing up in small Southern towns. The Carters acted like we were the ones with the Nobel Peace Prize. I wanted to vote for him again.

The only thing I had imagined President Carter saying that he actually said was, "Could we have our picture made with you?"

Having a saintly ex-president and first lady at church is a helpful reminder that worship is a big deal, but knowing God is in attendance ought to be enough.

Food and Family

Isn't it a shame that Jesus never went on a marriage retreat? (March 17, 2016)

Welcome to our Christian Marriage Enrichment Retreat! Good luck to all you happy couples! Calling it a "retreat" makes it sound like we are losing the war, but this weekend will be an attack on all the ways you are not who you ought to be as a couple!

We will be sharing Christ's love, but only with our spouses—ha! Here at the Christian Marriage Retreat Center, there are no televisions and no alcohol, so you get to spend two days with nothing but your beloved and your iPhone.

We will listen, listen, listen—except for the leaders, who will talk, talk, talk. We will explore your spiritual, physical, and emotional relationships in ways that will feel invasive at first, but by the end of the weekend will be merely unwarranted.

A huge thank you to Chelsea, who made the name tags with the adorable glittery wedding rings—which you are required to wear. If you are the special couple whose name tag has roses on the back, you get to be the first to tell us about the funny way you met. If you met at a bar or on Match.com, we encourage you to make up a story about meeting at church.

If your story is boring, you may feel better after we spend the first session talking about couples in the Bible. Boaz bought some land and got his wife as part of the deal. God told Hosea to marry a prostitute. King Solomon thought quantity was the way to go. One of the laws in Leviticus says that if your brother dies and you are male, then you have to marry his widow. Some of you are imagining that, and the hair is standing up on the back of your neck. This weekend, we will assume that Priscilla and Aquila met in a singles Sunday school class so we have one story to work with.

Jesus never went on a marriage retreat because he was perfect, so he could not get married. During our second session, we will look at what Jesus says about families. This will not take long.

Jesus says, "Whoever doesn't hate father and mother, wife and children, brothers and sisters, yes and even life itself, cannot be my disciple."

That's not a good verse to cross-stitch.

Jesus says, "I have come to set a man against his father, and a daughter against her mother, and a daughter-in-law against her mother-in-law; and one's enemies will be members of one's own household."

We wish Jesus would say one sentence about marriage that you could post on Facebook for Valentine's Day, but the Gospel writers must not have been paying enough attention.

You may enjoy the third session more, when we will sit in hula hoops looking into each other's eyes for an uncomfortable length of time. We will share intimate details and our deepest feelings. Everyone gets to write a love letter. You can mention sex during our discussions, but this is a Christian retreat, so we will giggle when you do.

During session four, we will tell you about the marriage-enriching things you are failing to do. We will be asking hard questions: Why is the garage his? Why doesn't he ever answer the phone? Why does he expect credit for every little thing he does around the house? Why is the bedroom hers? Why is she on her phone so much? Why doesn't she give him more credit for helping around the house? Why are these questions so sexist?

On Saturday morning, we will go hiking—the kind of activity that we can easily pretend to enjoy. We will be walking up a little hill, but we will keep calling it hiking up the mountain. Those who don't want to hike will play Married Pictionary, Married Catchphrase and The Newlywed Game, which are offered as incentives to hike up the mountain.

Saturday night is romantic movie night. The pastor asked us not to watch *Trainwreck* though she admits she hasn't seen it. The other choices are *Sleepless in Seattle* (the couple only has to get along for the last two minutes of the movie), *Groundhog Day* (it takes the guy a thousand tries to get it right) or *Silver Linings Playbook* (is it just me, or is he a little old for her?).

By the end of the weekend, you will either wonder how your parents stayed together without this retreat or know this weekend could have fixed your broken childhood.

We would like blueprints for the perfect marriage, but God gives us the wisdom to understand that there are no perfect couples. God gives us the grace to be kind long after the wedding bells have stopped ringing, the grace to be as polite to one another as we are to our friends, and the grace to keep our promises, even when it is hard.

"Amy Poehler is ruining my birthday!" Checking our secret desire to be famous (January 8, 2019)

On Saturday morning, I put on my hippest clothes and wished the holes were in different places. Our sons and I took my wife to a trendy breakfast spot in a trendy Brooklyn neighborhood for her birthday. I could have ordered seared, marinated tofu, but I went with scrambled eggs and toast. As we waited for Carol's beets with goat cheese and sweet roasted walnuts, we took turns naming things we love about Carol—her intelligence, her infectious laughter, her patience, her editing skills, her reasonable height, and her willingness to be the subject of other people's columns.

Then Amy Poehler came in. We are a *Parks and Rec* family. All of us would love to vote for Leslie Knope, the perky, mid-level bureaucrat in the Parks Department of Pawnee, a fictional town in Indiana we would have visited by now if it existed.

Ron Swanson is our favorite libertarian, Ann Perkins our favorite nurse, Andy Dwyer our favorite shoe-shiner, and Mouse Rat our favorite band. (We are the kind of fans who know that every Mouse Rat song includes one of these two lyrics: "Spread your wings and fly" or "You deserve to be a champion.")

Our family cried at Li'l Sebastian's Memorial Service. We imagine how sweet Sweetums must be. Leslie's hatred of libraries makes us question our love for libraries.

We have lived in New York long enough to know that when we see a celebrity, we do not acknowledge their fame. We do not touch them, talk to them, look them in the eye, ask for autographs, follow them into the bathroom, or take a picture. If the celebrity happens to be in a picture the waitress takes of your family that is just a coincidence. (You can see Amy just to the left of Graham's head.) When this happy coincidence happens, we do not share it, tweet it or Instagram it. We know stars are just people, so we are as chill as we can be, which is hard when the star is Amy Poehler. What is she eating? Leslie promised to "avoid salad and other disgusting things." Wouldn't it be great if she is eating waffles? Leslie taught us, "We have to remember what's important in life: friends, waffles, and work. Or waffles, friends, work. But work has to come third."

What if Amy Poehler says something to us? How should we respond? We do not want to say something she has heard a million times. Carol could say, "Ms. Poehler, Leslie was so right. My husband loves it when I show him I'm better than he is at something he loves." Amy might like it if we said, "We didn't want to bother you because Leslie taught us 'One person's annoying is another person's inspiring and heroic.'"

Amy Poehler and Graham, Caleb, Carol, and Brett Younger at breakfast

After several minutes of working on what we would say if Amy Poehler decided to join us at our table, Carol announced, "Amy Poehler is ruining my birthday!"

Carol was right. If we ignore the person at our table in favor of the celebrity two tables away, then we have a problem. A culture that suggests fame is the ultimate measure of success makes us feel bad that we do not look like Ryan Gosling. Plastic surgery seems reasonable. Reality TV passes for reality. Celebrity news looks like real news. If the mostly unknown believe that being mostly known is the goal that matters most, then they are not going to feel good about themselves.

When we become more interested in fame than reality, we need to put down *Us Weekly* and pick up the *New York Times*. We need to be able to name more senators than Real Housewives. We need to know more about the co-worker at the next desk than about Tom Brady.

When celebrities whine about being famous it seems ridiculous that they are complaining about achieving something so many people want, but they have a point. Fame does not usually lead to happiness. Celebrities often feel trapped by their fame.

Yet most of us harbor a secret desire to be famous. We crave the tiny reassurance of attention. We wait to be discovered. We are disappointed that we are not more celebrated.

Letting go of our desire to be famous could lead to better birthdays. Admiring people who do things worthy of our admiration—hard workers, loving parents, good listeners, caring teachers—could help us understand that anonymity is okay. The happiest person could be a perky, mid-level bureaucrat who enjoys life and a good breakfast.

Eating burgers, sinning boldly (February 8, 2018)

If you are leaving New York to visit Texas, these are socially acceptable comments:

• "I could use some warm weather."
• "We're looking forward to seeing friends."
• "I miss driving more than 30 miles an hour."
• "I haven't seen an armadillo in a long time."
• "I enjoy the jealousy on people's faces when I say 'I'm from Brooklyn.'"

This is not a socially acceptable comment: "I want a Quarter Pounder with fries."

I know how unsophisticated that makes me sound. After two years in a culinary mecca, a center for gastronomic delights and the world's best pizza, I am supposed to be beyond mass-produced fast food, but I am not. Mine is not a sophisticated palate.

This is a difficult confession to make. I know how bad ordering off the dollar menu is. I saw *Supersize Me*. Finger lickin' good is not good for me. I can see that the Burger King is creepy. I have read studies that say if you eat a bacon cheeseburger, you have a 75 percent chance of a heart attack before you get to the Frosty.

But I live 250 miles from the nearest Cook Out. None of the arguments against driving through a drive-thru—and staring at the menu until the guy behind me starts honking—are enough to keep my mouth from watering with anticipation at driving south on Interstate 35 knowing there are six fast food places at every exit.

Fast food is democratic. Working people can afford everything that you stand in line to order—and you do not have to tip. There are no surprises. Every Whataburger tastes exactly like the Whataburger you had five years ago at the Whataburger 500 miles away. Why have it your way when you can have it the same way every time?

I do not know how to explain to New Yorkers that fast food fountain drinks are better. Free refills are a right guaranteed somewhere deep in the Constitution. A liter of Coca-Cola from a grocery store is a pale imitation of a Cherry Coke at Sonic. Anyone who has had the pleasure of eating a meal in their car at a Sonic Drive-In knows there is no better ice in all the world.

No one asks, "Are we dressed well enough?" before going to Dairy Queen. No one worries that their preschoolers might act up at Subway. Children do not get a toy with their meal at Ruth Chris Steak House. There is no playground at Del Frisco's.

Brett Younger, sinning boldly

As I sat on the plane heading to Dallas, I thought about the options: Whataburger's Honey Butter Chicken Biscuit (sugar and butter make food wonderful); Jack in the Box's two-for-$1 tacos, the perfect level of greasiness; KFC's original recipe anything; the chicken sandwich at Chick-fil-A (the pickle chips are the key); an Oreo blizzard at Dairy Queen (Oreo crumbs are to ice cream what bacon is to everything else).

I ended up thinking inside the bun—a Homestyle Burger (an ironic name) and an iced mocha. This is nothing to write home about, but I'm lovin' it. I know that if they served a McDonald's iced mocha at Starbucks, it would cost twice as much.

When Martin Luther wrote, "Love God and sin boldly," he was not in a fast food restaurant, but he could have been. Luther was inviting us to recognize what is important and what is not. Sometimes you should order the salad, but sinning a little without worrying about it too much may, on occasion, be good for your soul.

As Lent approaches, some of us are deciding whether to give up soft drinks, sugar, or Nacho Cheese Doritos Locos Tacos Supreme. We would do better to give up envy, anger, or greed. We have many things about which we should feel guilty—how little we give to feed hungry people, how quickly we dismiss people who dismiss us, and how much time we spend on our own amusement. Because there is so much about which we should feel guilty, we can feel free—every now and then—to eat curly fries boldly.

Holy smoke: Barbecue with a side of faith (August 4, 2016)

I think of my vegetarian friends like I think of my Jewish friends. I love and respect them, but we are of different faiths. I believe in barbecue.

To the casual observer those who gather for a church barbecue have found an excuse to overeat, but to serious students of the Bible and church history, we are doing God's work.

Deuteronomy 12:15 says, "Yet whenever you desire you may slaughter and eat meat within any of your towns, according to the blessing that the Lord your God has given you; the unclean and the clean may eat of it."

You may want to crochet Deuteronomy 12:20 on an apron for a beloved carnivore: "When the Lord your God enlarges your territory, as God has promised you, and you say, 'I am going to eat some meat,' because you wish to eat meat, you may eat meat whenever you have the desire."

Ezekiel 24:10 was written by a prophet who knows his way around a pit: "Heap up the logs, kindle the fire, cook the meat well, mix in the spices, and let the bones be burned."

This is the Word of the Lord. Thanks be to God.

Food is more than a means of sustenance. The Old Testament is filled with dietary laws, cooking instructions, and Martha Stewart-like details on what to eat during holidays. The royal feast is the primary image of the coming kingdom of God. Isaiah describes the messianic banquet: "The Lord of Hosts will make for all peoples a feast of rich food, a feast of well-aged wine, of rich food filled with marrow" (25:6).

The menu for the kingdom banquet varies from church to church. More lime Jell-O is sold in Utah than in any other state because Latter-day Saints take it to potluck dinners. Greek Orthodox churches are famous for baklava. Catholics still eat fish on Friday. The bread at Episcopal gatherings is likely to be fresh-baked—from an upscale French bakery.

Barbecue brings a variety of Christians together. The perfect combination of smoke, meat, and fire creates a meal and a moment when we taste and see that God is good.

Church barbecue has a long, rich history. In the first half of the nineteenth century, evangelists enticed crowds to camp meetings with scented smoke and sizzling meats. Before restaurants like Porky's Last Stand, Adam's Rib and Bubba Lou's Bodacious BBQ, you could not order one barbecue sandwich. You ate barbecue only when an entire animal was cooked. In order to avoid waste, everyone was welcome at a barbecue. Revival barbecue was one of the few times there was more than enough food.

Barbecue is a religious experience—especially in African American churches in the South. In Texas, there are church-connected barbecue restaurants, like New Zion Missionary Baptist Church Barbecue in Huntsville. Pit masters are called "preachers" and their barbecue pits "pulpits" from which the holy word is served.

Some barbecue joints try to avoid the sectarian divisions that divide the barbecue belt and claim to serve "nondenominational barbecue." They do not see that the divisions—Kansas City, Memphis, North Carolina, South Carolina, and Texas—are denominations making distinctive contributions. (All should, however, agree that liquid smoke is an abomination.)

God creates the low, indirect heat that produces hickory-smoked baby-back ribs. Watching someone combine science and art in the act of barbecuing—the expectation, the understanding that you do not really want the meat to fall off the bone, and the savoring of each bite—is a means by which a church becomes a better church. Barbecue should be served with a side of faith and a prayer that barbecue will be served in the afterlife. Is it too much to say that barbecue is to Christians what the Passover lamb is to the Jews? (Yes, it is too much to say.)

Robert Capon said of a fellow he knew who was counting calories: "His body may or may not lose weight. His soul, however, is sure to wither."

Barbecue keeps our souls from withering.

In a 1902 article about a Methodist church barbecue in Denver, Columbus Hill, a pit master who understood the spiritual aspects of barbecue, said, "This method of serving meat is descended from the sacrificial altars of the time of Moses when the priests of the temple got their fingers greasy and dared not wipe them on their Sunday clothes. They discovered then the rare, sweet taste of meat flavored with the smoke of its own juices."

Praise the Lord and pass the sauce.

Anthony Bourdain, Kate Spade, my grandmother, and bad theology (June 20, 2018)

My favorite grandmother took her own life in 1950—eleven years before I was born. My other grandmothers were fine (my father's father provided me with four grandmothers), but my father's mother is my favorite.

I have a tiny photograph in my desk drawer. My grandmother is leaning on the fender of a 1930s Plymouth coupe—the kind Warren Beatty drove in *Bonnie and Clyde*. She is wearing a white dress and high heel pumps. Her hair looks like it is bobby pinned.

Ruth Sharp Younger

She is an attractive woman in her twenties, trying unsuccessfully to smile. Maybe she is looking into the sun, or perhaps she cannot quite figure out how to smile. My grandmother suffered from depression at a time when mental illness was less understood and medication was woefully inadequate.

She has been my favorite grandmother since I learned that she wrote a novel. Most of my ancestors, including the Methodist preacher, the horse thief, and the railroad boss who "was never convicted of murdering anyone," were not big on books. I find it hard to imagine my relatives reading books, much less writing them. When my family members went fishing or hunting and I wanted to stay home and read, I thought, "Grandmother Ruth would understand."

I have thought about what I would say, if I could, to this wounded woman whose genes I carry: "You have a grandson on the way who wants to meet you and talk about books and writing. You can't imagine the people who will need you someday."

When my parents asked what I wanted for Christmas one year, I requested a copy of my grandmother's novel. You do not have to read far to understand why it was never published. The story is painfully autobiographical. She describes in dark detail the deaths of two of her children.

In one of many anguished passages she blames herself as well as God. She believes that her baby died because she "clung to the doubt that was forever in the back of my mind."

As the death of a second child approaches, her mother, the daughter of a Baptist preacher, says, "I can only hope and pray and be ready to reconcile myself to whatever is God's will."

My grandmother responds, "If the baby dies, do you think that God will be treating me right?"

"God treats everyone right, you know that."

God must cringe when a well-meaning person speaks such blasphemy. No one in the novel ever suggests that God weeps for every grieving parent or that it is not God's will for children to die. I do not know all of the reasons my grandmother took her life, but I feel certain that bad theology contributed to her death.

I have been thinking about my grandmother since the suicides of Kate Spade and Anthony Bourdain. Their deaths have brought much-needed attention to the growing epidemic of suicides. Some of the fatalities were victims of bad theology. Some never heard a helpful word from the church.

Mental illness is complicated, and the church does not have all of the answers. At the very least, the church has to speak loudly and clearly of God's love, mercy, and liberation.

I wish someone had said this to my grandmother before she died far too soon: "We can't imagine the pain you feel, but God can. God grieves with us. You can hold on because God is holding on to you."

A word of hope might have changed the ending.

Six words to describe a life: Saints don't know they are saints (February 20, 2015)

As a child of deaf parents, she was the one who made the phone call when the refrigerator stopped working. Bennie went to bed knowing she was the one who would hear if something happened during the night. Listening for her parents gave her not only a sense of responsibility, but also a concern for others. My mother-in-law loved everyone in the room, but she cared most for the one who felt left out.

Bennie gave herself to making the church a home for everyone. She pushed congregations toward the fierce love of Christ. She was a social worker without the title.

In Alexandria, Virginia, she saw deaf people being left out and started a deaf ministry. Bennie interpreted the sermons of her husband, Vernon Davis, into sermons for the deaf congregation. Most of the time she translated. Sometimes she edited on the fly.

When she and Vernon moved first to Midwestern Seminary and then to the Logsdon School of Theology, she continued to look after those who might be overlooked. She was around people who know how to talk about faith, but Bennie instinctively knew that our theology needs to move beyond the words we say to become the compassion with which we live.

One afternoon, she and Vernon were stuck in Kansas City traffic when they saw a disheveled woman walking down the highway, barefoot, carrying her high heels. A car in front of them stopped, and a man shouted for the woman to get into the car, but she wouldn't go near him. Bennie, of course, insisted they offer the woman help. The woman explained that she came to Kansas City for a party that got out of hand and she had to leave. The woman wanted to go home, three hours away.

Midwestern had a few short-term apartments, so Vernon offered to let her stay the night there, but the woman said she had to get home. They checked on public transportation, but no bus was heading that way. The woman decided she wanted to get out of the car and try her luck getting a ride. Bennie, of course, insisted they drive her all the way home. Vernon remembered his more grudging generosity because he had to get up the next morning and drive another three hours to preach a sermon.

That is enough to make it a good story, but Bennie kept in touch with the woman. They corresponded. Bennie checked in from time to time to make sure the woman was doing OK. If you were stuck on the side of the road, you hoped Bennie was in the next car.

Unlike most of us, most of the time, Bennie did not *act* like she was concerned for others. She *was* concerned. She did not act like a good person. She was a good person. She did not act like a Christian. She was a Christian.

Compassion was in the air around her. She taught her children to care for others. I live with Bennie every day. I am reminded of her every time my wife, Carol, makes me care for someone I do not care for or give away something I would rather keep. My life would be less Christian without Bennie.

I lost so much with her passing, but I have been given so much that I cannot lose. I feel like I have lost the 81-year-old whose days had become so hard, but I cannot lose the woman who came to Louisville to check out a prospective son-in-law and was quite direct about it. We went to dinner and, as part of the interview process, I was called on to pray. I inadvertently thanked God for family. Bennie said, "Brett, I'm glad you mentioned family. That's what we want to talk about." Family was often what she wanted to talk about. Bennie gave herself to the family to which God calls us.

On St. Valentine's Day, at Bennie's funeral at First Baptist Church in Austin, we felt invited to trust the God who gave Bennie courage as she cared for her parents, the God who led Bennie to the love of her life—her husband for 59 years—the God who took Bennie to a place where deaf people needed her help to worship, the God who shared Bennie with seminaries where she cared for students, faculty and staff, and the God who filled her with compassion and helped her teach that compassion to others. We can trust the God who through the saints calls us to a better way.

Seminary Life

Confessions of a seminary professor (June 12, 2015)

A seminary faculty posted a photo on Facebook with the caption: "Our faculty and all of the books they have written." The faculty is made up of superb scholars who have authored a huge stack of books, but you wonder if a sarcastic person might suggest a different caption. Jesus addressed his disciples, "The religion scholars are fine teachers. Follow their teachings but be careful about following them. They enjoy talking about their faculty positions and hearing the flattery of students. They love being called 'Doctor.'" (This is a loose paraphrase of Matthew 23 by someone whose knowledge of Greek would not qualify him for a faculty position.)

I confess that I like having my picture taken with the books I have written. I love the diplomas on my wall. I love processing in my robe and stole. I even love the tam that makes me look like a pastry chef in the French Navy.

Followers of Christ are to become uninterested in position, prestige, or publicity—even if they are seminary professors.

I need to confess when I try to impress the educated rather than care for the underprivileged.

I need to confess when I act as if I should be measured by how many know my name rather than by Christ's priorities.

I need to confess when I would rather add a line to my resume than spend time helping a church.

I need to confess when I do anything meant to make me look good rather than contribute to Christ's kingdom.

Seminary professors warn students that the institution of the church is only the means to the end of serving God. Those same professors are in danger of treating the academy as the end rather than the means to serve. We sin when we do not hear Jesus ask Nicodemus, "Are you a teacher of Israel and yet you do not understand?"

We can do better. The academy can serve the church, but not when we serve the academy. Rather than focusing on impressing other scholars, professors should give more to God.

Student evaluations and ratemyprofessor.com make professors feel more like competitors than teachers, but professors can be mentors. Most seminary graduates forget the kings of Judah, the dates of the Great

Awakenings, and how to translate the periphrastic perfect passive participle, but we cling to the memory of a teacher who loved God and taught us to love God, too.

Seminary professors should do their jobs in a way that makes no sense if we do not believe in Christ. We understand that it is hard to quantify the best moments of what we do. The more important something is the harder it is to measure.

I should stop just telling students to follow Jesus and try to show them how.

I should make it clear that the purpose of theological education is not knowing more information than others know but becoming more like Christ.

I should stop trying to give young ministers the tools to climb the ecclesiological ladder and give them instead the perspective to wonder what the ladder is leaning against and leading to.

Seminary professors need to keep their doors open to talk about things that matter. Professors need to ask students, "What is God doing in your life? What are you up against? What feels like a gift? What are your hopes for the church? Can I pray with you?"

Seminary professors need to invite students into their homes because Christians do that. We need to make it clear that a student's GPA matters less than experiencing God's grace. We need to work beyond the syllabus to encourage students to ask big questions.

Seminary professors need to be patient with students who come only for the degree and celebrate the ones who come because they adore Jesus. We need to help students understand that seminary should be less about preparing for a career than becoming a servant of Christ.

Karl Barth said, "Nowhere is the grace of God more evident than in the fact that some preachers will be saved"—even ones who like being called "Doctor." Seminary professors need to love God and their neighbor. Sometimes that will mean writing a book about it.

Seminaries reluctantly selling their souls (November 25, 2015)

When I was sixteen, I inexplicably got a job as a mechanic. I was assigned to tires and batteries—the kindergarten of the automotive world. Even in the department in which I could do the least damage, I was a problem. Flat tires I repaired came back flat. New batteries I put in acted like old batteries. (Diehards died easily in my hands.) I installed one muffler that did not muffle. I was not trusted around brakes. I pray that I did not hurt anyone.

After a week of other mechanics repairing my repairs, the manager took me aside. "Brett," he said, "we don't want bad things to happen, so you're now a student in our automotive repair correspondence program. You get a ten cent an hour raise for each test you pass. You make more money and the customers stay alive. Everybody wins."

A week later I was making sixty cents more an hour, but I still could not work a pair of pliers. It wasn't until the manager ordered real mechanics to work with me that I learned to fix cars. They stuck their head under the same hood, showed me how to do it, and answered my questions. We do not want mechanics, doctors, firefighters, police officers, or ministers who have prepared with only a workbook.

Seminaries are dealing with difficult questions about how to prepare ministers. The number of Master of Divinity students in the United States decreased six percent last year. When seminaries struggle financially, they are tempted to offer online versions of correspondence courses. The majority of the small number of seminaries that are growing are doing so by offering online degrees. New degree programs and new delivery systems are attempts to meet the demand for cheaper diplomas, fewer classes, and less sacrifice. Many students who study online are juggling work and family responsibilities, but for others it is about expediency.

We need to recognize what we give up when we whittle down require-ments. Degrees that cost less to obtain may cost more in the long run.

Financial challenges make it difficult for seminaries to keep asking important questions: What kind of teaching will best serve Christ's church? How can we give students the kind of learning experience they can share in their ministries? Where is the Spirit leading? What would God have us do?

Reading books and taking quizzes is a fine way to learn facts, but we need relationships to learn to live as the church. Even when the technology is amazing, the teachers are not sticking their heads under the same hood. Students sit at their computers watching lectures that the professors deliv-ered to previous students. The professors miss the confused look on the student's face as well as the "aha" moment of shared discovery.

Many students complain about online classes. They recognize that this is not the best preparation to serve. Students who attend classes in person find it hard not to resent those who receive the same degree without making the same sacrifices. Students who wish they could meet with their professor and other students are denied the opportunity when the class they need is only offered online. The trend in theological education to require less of students will, in time, hurt the church. Is it really a seminary education if we are not worshiping together, praying with one another, or talking about Jesus between classes?

My experience as a seminary student was less about memorizing content than about being transformed by teachers who shared themselves. I do not remember many dates from church history, but I remember Bill Leonard working hard to convince us that the history of the church could lead us to love the church. I am fuzzy about whether Karl Barth was from Switzerland or Germany, but I remember when Frank Tupper talked about the problem of evil with a heart so broken that our hearts broke, too. I cannot tell you the name of every textbook Raymond Bailey assigned, but when my wife, Carol, suffered a miscarriage, Raymond and his wife, Pat, drove an hour to pray with us.

When people argue for online education they often say, "It's almost like being in the same room," but "almost" is not as good. Some students and young professors will never know how good a seminary education can be.

Students can learn online. Friendships can form online. God can be heard through computer speakers, but it is hard to imagine the Lord's Supper as a Skype meeting.

White preaching professor, black preaching students (September 20, 2013)

George Shine III, Dihanne Moore, and Joshua Scott are three of the best and brightest at the McAfee School of Theology. We sat down to talk about seminary, race, and what would happen if I preached in their churches.

Brett: Our student body is 48 percent African American and 13 of the 15 faculty members are white. Have you wondered if this is a good place for an African American minister?

Dihanne: What really shocked me was the first time I went to chapel. I thought, "Oh no! I can't do this. They're singing hymns out of a hymnal. Nobody's saying 'Amen!' Nobody's shouting, 'Hallelujah!'" I made myself go and ended up embracing a new way to worship God. It's just different.

Brett: Are you glad you are at a racially diverse seminary?

George: I wouldn't have it any other way because that's the real world. You have to learn how to deal with people that are different from you, and you might as well learn that here.

Joshua: My breakthrough came in preaching. Now I feel comfortable saying, "It doesn't matter who's out there. I can reach them with the word of God." That's when I said, "McAfee was not a mistake."

Brett: What do you wish African American churches knew about seminary?

Joshua: That it's not the devil. That you can go to a multicultural seminary and not lose your African Americanness.

George: My church is concerned that you're going to lose what they've taught you. They're afraid that the professors are going to teach you what to believe and not just how to better interpret the word of God.

Dihanne: My pastor encourages us to go to seminary. She wants all of her ministers to be trained theologically: "When you go to seminary you don't want to lose your mind. Don't let them beat the Spirit out of you, but at the same time, education broadens your horizons and opens you up to read the word."

Brett: Are African American churches requiring seminary in a way they wouldn't have twenty years ago?

George: It's becoming, and I hate to use this word, competitive. Every church looks at other churches: "This preacher has letters behind his name. We need to get somebody like that so that we can attract the younger generation."

Joshua: You are not able to preach "Jesus wept" and whoop the rest of the time. They want meat in the sermon. They want to know, "What does this say and mean?" The bar has been raised. You are going to have to go dip in the pool that is seminary.

Dihanne: Some of the older saints don't believe that you've preached until you've whooped! It's almost as if you could say, "I went down to the corner store," and a few people would shout, "Hallelujah!" The younger people don't want to hear the whooping and hollering. They are searching for something deeper.

Joshua: For young preachers coming up, you've got to do it all. I'm a whooper, but I give you everything. I give you all the exegetical stuff you want and then for my people, Mama and them, I bring you the cross.

Dihanne: At the end of it, you have to have the celebration moment or you didn't preach.

Brett: How do white professors misunderstand black preaching?

George: I think they confuse our emotions with showing off. They don't understand the hurt and the pain that the members are bringing. You have to preach to their pain. We expect a preacher to understand what we're going through. I've got to be emotional to let them know that I hear them.

Joshua: But I think it goes deeper. It comes from an inherited point of view, from slavery. We identify with the children of Israel. We say, "God did it for them. God will do it for us." When Barack Obama became president, the old people wanted to celebrate every single Sunday because you've got something to shout about now. You don't sit in the back, and at the counter nobody's throwing hot coffee in your face. When they think about all that, it makes them shout and run and holler and whoop a little bit. They expect it every Sunday.

Dihanne: When we say "praise God" in a black church, we're not looking for silent meditation. We expect exuberant praise because we understand the oppression we have overcome.

Brett: So how would it go if I preached at your church?

George: I would get a lot of questions afterwards.

Joshua: At your conclusion they would ask, "Is that it?" but they would be very nice to you and talk about you once you left.

George: I don't believe that just anyone can come in and preach to black people. You may be able to perform on *American Idol,* but that does not mean you are going to make it at the Apollo.

Dihanne: I think you would do well at our church. Some of the members would appreciate getting out in time for lunch.

Brett: I might do better than you think.

George: We'll help you.

Brett: What might I hear if it was going well?

George: "Amen!"

Dihanne: "Come on with it!"

Brett: And if it isn't going well?

Dihanne: Silence.

George: It's terrible if nobody says anything.

Brett: What's a bad move for a white preacher in an African American church?

George: Acting black.

Joshua: We can tell it's not you hollering at the top of your lungs. Just be yourself.

George: It's like a white comedian trying to tell black jokes. Don't mention Michael Jackson.

Brett: That sounds like good advice.

How seminaries fail (November 22, 2013)

A light shines on them. A voice calls their name. The Spirit ignites their hearts. They feel compelled to follow Jesus, challenge the church, and change the world. They long to proclaim good news to the poor, release to the captives, and recovery of sight to the blind.

They tell someone about their call to serve Christ and are told to go to seminary, so they move far from their homes, friends, and jobs. They pray, plan, and commit three years and considerable expense because their souls are on fire.

New students show up on the first day of class ready to take up a cross and die for their faith. Then faculty members begin teaching them to exegete 2 Timothy, conjugate Greek verbs, and compare and contrast Calvinism and Arminianism. Students learn to trace the lineage of the kings of Israel, argue about the doctrine of the Trinity, and preach clever, inoffensive sermons.

At our worst, seminaries invite disciples to scholarship that forgets its purpose. The impression given is that God's grace is so complicated that you have to have a master's degree to share it.

Teachers who have not been on a church staff since the 1980s inadvertently increase the distance between the seminary and the church. Professors become so sophisticated that they are reticent to talk about giving their hearts to Jesus.

At our worst, we calm down John the Baptist. We turn down the volume. We pour water on the fire. We teach students to weigh the alternatives.

At our worst, the house next door is on fire and seminaries are teaching students to trim the hedges. The car is about to fly over the cliff and seminaries are changing the radio station. Children have nothing to eat and seminaries are teaching students to look like good ministers.

Too many students learn to be as careful, effective, and political as Pharisees. They graduate from seminary and find a safe institution that will help pay off the debt they have accrued. They spend their ministries rearranging deck chairs on the Titanic, fiddling while Rome burns, and handing out aspirins while the world explodes.

Our seminaries can do better. Our classrooms start the day as empty boxes. The professor's job is to be an instrument by which God fills those rooms with passion, joy, and revolution. Seminary can be an electric gathering if we believe that love makes a difference, hope can be reawakened, and evil can be overcome by living like Christ.

We exegete 2 Timothy to hear God calling us to "fight a good fight, finish the course and keep the faith." We learn to conjugate Greek verbs because we need to take Jesus' words seriously enough to struggle to understand them. We need to recognize John Calvin's narrowness so that we will more fully celebrate the wideness of God's mercy.

We read about the kings of Israel because God invites us to dance like David did. We argue about the Trinity because we have experienced the Spirit in surprising ways. We preach because the world lies and someone needs to tell the truth.

At our best, seminaries invite disciples to a deeper faith. We talk about how Christ transformed us because we cannot help but speak of what God has done.

At our best, seminary is a gathering of those who search for the meaning of life, join with others on the journey, and ask God to show us where love leads. Students and teachers teach one another to be courageous.

At our best, we learn to want what God wants. We worry about what God worries about. We weep over what God weeps over. We push for what God pushes for.

Seminaries should not focus on ministers being efficient, effective, and successful. The church needs fervor, anger, and desire.

Seminaries should not produce ministers who want to maintain the church. The church needs ministers who will poke and prod the church.

Seminaries should not encourage self-serving ministers. The church needs ministers who will set their own hair on fire for what is right.

Seminaries have created enough predictable, conventional, cookie-cutter ministers. The church needs ardent, zealous, incensed, enraged, and impassioned ministers.

Seminaries should be converting temple administrators into St. Francis, Martin Luther, Lottie Moon, Dietrich Bonhoeffer, and Mother Teresa.

Seminaries should be blessing faithful outliers, nonconformists, mavericks, eccentrics, and dissenters. The church has enough people keeping rules. God needs exceptions to the rules.

Seminaries need to help ministers do the things Jesus did—feed the hungry, listen to the lonely, and heal the broken.

Seminaries should not be satisfied training students to maintain institutions. At our best, seminaries are a way God stirs ministers, turns up the volume, and throws gasoline on the fire.

Leaving Fred Craddock's funeral, yearning just to be Christian (March 20, 2015)

I was early to Fred Craddock's funeral. Cherry Log Christian Church is less than two hours from Atlanta, but a trip to Appalachia seemed farther, so I gave myself way too much time. I had been told to eat at the Pink Pig barbecue restaurant, but it is only open Thursday to Sunday. I had, however, brought an autographed book to read as we waited for the service to begin. *Craddock Stories* is a collection of Fred's greatest hits. Preaching aficionados identify the stories with a phrase, "the church voted 234-2," "playing hide and seek," "the lady in the grocery store who thinks he's hitting on her," "poor as Job's turkey," and "Jesus winning the Georgia football game."

Fred Craddock changed preaching. He grew up with preachers who filled sanctuaries with three points, multiple sub points, and a poem to encapsulate the boredom. These preachers told us what they were going to tell us, told us, and then recapped what they had told us without noticing that we stopped listening after the first summary. Fred realized that what keeps most of us from living for Jesus is not a lack of information. He invited preachers to stop teaching the lessons of Scripture and start telling the stories of faith. These stories, he argued, do not illustrate the point because they are the point.

When he was twenty, Craddock went to hear Albert Schweitzer. His plan was to criticize Schweitzer's *Quest for the Historical Jesus*, but before he had a chance, Schweitzer invited Craddock to go with him to help the dying in Africa. Fred said, "I learned, again, what it means to be Christian and had hopes that I could be that someday."

Craddock's first pastorate was near Oak Ridge, Tennessee. When the little town boomed, the church voted not to follow Fred's recommendation that they reach out to the new residents. Years later, after telling his wife that painful story, they went to see the little church. They were surprised to find the parking lot full. A great big sign said, "Barbecue, all you can eat." Fred said to Nettie, "It's a good thing this is not still a church, otherwise these people couldn't be here."

When Craddock was a young pastor, one church told him he had an emergency fund with $100 in it. He could give the money to anybody with a need that is not the result of "laziness, drunkenness, or poor management." Fred asked, "What else is there?" He figured they still have the money.

Fred told some stories you wish you had not heard. He was teaching at Phillips Theological Seminary when a woman brought her dying brother to be healed. Craddock said, "I can pray for him, but I do not have the gift of healing." She responded, "Then what in the world do you do?" Fred said, "What I did that afternoon was study, stare at my books, and try to forget what she said."

A woman a few pews in front of me had come to the funeral with the same book of stories and the same idea I had. It is easier to cry before the service begins because no one is paying attention.

We sang "Soon we'll reach the shining river." Fred's daughter Laura spoke with deep affection of waiting with dread for her father to mention her in a sermon: "O God, what is he going to say?" His son John, who is much bigger than Fred, said he liked it when his father called him "a block off the old chip."

We heard Paul's promise that "nothing can separate us from the love of God in Christ Jesus our Lord." Tom Long preached, imagining Lloyd Bentsen saying, "I served with Fred Craddock. I knew Fred Craddock. Fred Craddock was a friend of mine. You are no Fred Craddock." But Tom made us think about Fred and the God who holds us all. We closed the beautiful, modest service with an Appalachian folk hymn, "And when from death I'm free I'll sing on, I'll sing on."

Fred Craddock wrote, "When I was in my late teens, I wanted to be a preacher. When I was in my late twenties, I wanted to be a good preacher. Now that I am older, I want more than anything else to be a Christian. To live simply, to love generously, to speak truthfully, to serve faithfully, and to leave everything else to God."

I left Fred Craddock's funeral wanting to be a Christian.

My speech to seminary graduates (April 21, 2014)

Once again, no seminary has chosen me to give the speech at their graduation service. My mother and I do not get it. We both feel like I am the perfect person to hand out the kind of inspirational hooey that young ministers need on their big day.

I would do a good job of droning on about how the word commencement means "to begin," and so this is not the end of something but the beginning of a lifelong journey of ministry, a time of marching to the beat of our own drums, taking the road less traveled, lighting candles rather than cursing the darkness, and following our hearts. I can tell them that ministry will be wonderful and that ministry will be hard. They need to do ministry in old ways and they need to throw out the old ways of doing ministry. The church needs more poets and the last thing the church needs is another poet. I had begun a rough draft just in case:

Prominent president, illustrious dean, weary faculty, absent alumni, distinguished trustees, assorted rich people—write a check and you can be a distinguished trustee—I am grateful for the lack of judgment that led to this invitation. Congratulations, graduating seminary students. Today you get more initials after your name and an extra line in your obituary. Your parents are proud, and your loan officer is waiting. Your seminary has prepared you to make very little money.

But this is the day the crowd goes wild—mint juleps on the infield, Bubba Watson putting on the green jacket, and you leading the parade, high-stepping it in front of a brass band—trumpets, trombones and tubas, smiling like the pope on Easter.

We have set this day aside to applaud and remember.

Remember the students you met in Spiritual Formation who did not seem like they belonged in seminary any more than you do.

Remember debating whether you should preach like your professor taught you if you are in shorts and sandals at youth camp.

Remember the look on your teacher's face when a student—now a former student—asked, "Instead of Paul Tillich, can I read Joel Osteen for my book review?"

Remember wanting to turn to the person next to you and ask, "Did you know the animals wouldn't fit in the ark?" but you were smart enough to keep it to yourself.

Remember how you wanted to raise your hand to say that your pastor back home has a different idea about the Book of Revelation.

Remember all the books by dead people that they made you read. You wished Augustine had seen a therapist, Brother Lawrence had gotten out of the kitchen once in a while, and Teresa of Avila had received the medication she so clearly needed.

Remember when you started to get it.

Remember when you began hoping to see particular people on the first day of class.

Remember the first time you changed your mind because you were here.

Remember reading a passage in Ezekiel and thinking, "I didn't know that was in the Bible. I'm not sure that should be in the Bible."

Remember wondering why the pastoral care professor said you should never sit on a hospital bed. One day you will try it and realize she was right.

Remember falling in love with the church again.

Remember the capstone class that *almost* made you wish it wasn't over.

Remember, because now it is time to go make a difference.

Go, lead the church to be more like Jesus than most have imagined a church can be.

Go, lead the church to learn the stories of faith for the purpose of becoming faithful followers.

Go, lead the church to care for one another, share their hopes and dreams, and become sisters and brothers in Christ.

Go, lead the church to overcome the boundaries of race and economics, filled with warm hearts and open minds.

Go, lead the church to honestly look for truth because we are looking for the one who is truth.

Go, lead the church to take the past seriously because it takes the future seriously, to call for authentic worship, costly discipleship, and genuine ministry.

Go, lead the church to become better followers of Jesus.

If the church is so great, then why are you teaching in seminary? (May 12, 2016)

During my first class as a professor at Mercer University's McAfee School of Theology, I began waxing poetic on my years as a pastor and the glory of preaching: "What could be more wonderful than to imagine your way back into the biblical world, to listen for what the Spirit is saying to your congregation—people you love—and stand up on Sunday morning to say, 'I have been listening carefully and I think this is what God wants us to hear'?"

A student asked, "If the church is so great, then why are you here?"

For eight years I have been working on that good, rude question. I love teaching, so I am finding it hard to leave McAfee to become the pastor of Plymouth Church in Brooklyn, New York. (If the disrespectful student is reading this, I hope you feel bad.)

For three weeks I have been humming *Mr. Holland's Opus*. Do you remember the scene where the student says, "We are your symphony, Mr. Holland. We are the melodies and the notes. We are the music of your life."

I imagine a student saying, "We are your sermons, Dr. Younger. We are the examples and illustrations. We are the sermons of your life."

This has not happened.

One of the ways I am dealing with my grief is to make a list of things I am glad to leave behind.

I will not miss students arguing that they should not be counted absent on the first day of class because they had not yet signed up for the course.

I will not miss students saying, "I am going to be late with my sermon because the internet is down."

I will not miss this conversation: "Dr. Younger, you can't give me a C. The Holy Spirit gave me this sermon." ("The Spirit gets an A. You got a C.")

I will not miss multiple choice, true-false, fill-in-the-blank, or wild guesses.

I will not miss grading book reviews that begin, "Anna Carter Florence's *Preaching as Testimony* is a nine-year-old book written by Anna Carter Florence in 2007."

I will not miss students thinking I need to listen to a sermon by Joel Osteen.

I will not miss assessment reports. I will never again write, "19 out of 21 students in the worship class were able to identify 16 out of 20 worship terms from the 17th and 18th centuries."

I will not miss faculty meetings that focus on enrollment: "Can we devise an MDiv that does not require reading? How can we recruit wealthy students? How can we schedule courses so that students can get a degree while only being on campus from 7 to 10 p.m. one Friday a month?"

Reading my list of things I will not miss might suggest that I am glad to leave my present occupation, but the list of things I will miss is much longer.

I will miss faculty meetings when we ask good questions: "How can we take seriously 2,000 years of church history as well as the churches that our students need to start? How do we center what we do in the story of Jesus? What would God have us do?"

I will miss being a member of a faculty that reads Scripture with thoughtfulness, believes in the goodness of God, and knows that God is bigger than we think.

I will miss the six weeks of summer when there are no classes.

I will miss being delighted to see students on the first day of class.

I will miss reading book reviews that begin, "Anna Carter Florence needs to visit Second Baptist Church, Lime Sink, Georgia, before she writes another book."

I will miss students thinking I need to hear a sermon by Barbara Brown Taylor.

I will miss moments when it was not about the grade, but about Jesus. Moments in preaching when a student said something none of us had heard before. Moments in worship when we felt the presence of the Spirit.

I will miss students changing their minds—and changing my mind.

I will miss students saying, "The Jesus in the Gospels is a lot more complicated than what I learned in Sunday school, but I like this Jesus more. I want to follow this Jesus."

I will miss students believing the church can be more like Christ than most churches have ever been.

I will miss students caring for one another, sharing their hopes and dreams, and becoming sisters and brothers.

I will miss arguing over tough questions.

I will miss students overcoming the boundaries of gender, race, and sexual orientation.

I will miss students who are ardent, zealous, fervent, fiery, incensed, and impassioned.

I will miss students who are outliers, nonconformists, mavericks, eccentrics, dissidents, and dissenters.

I will miss the followers of Christ who called me their teacher.

Santiago, Chile

Felices son los estupidos (July 18, 2014)

"Once in your life before you die you ought to see a country where they don't talk in English and don't even want to." Mrs. Gibbs's recommendation in *Our Town* has stuck with me, so Carol and I are serving for five months in Chile as the interim ministers at Santiago Community Church, a delightful, international, interdenominational, English-speaking congregation in a decidely non-English speaking country.

I prepared before we came to Chile. I read *Spanish Made Easy*. I played a Spanish Word game on my phone that really wants me to know the verb *brotar*. (Apparently a lot of sprouting goes on in the Spanish-speaking world.) I listened to thirty podcasts from Johnny Spanish, who promised to help me learn Spanish "crazy fast."

I felt confident, but, in retrospect, I missed some warning signs even before we left Georgia.

I went to the bank teller whose name tag said, "*Yo hablo espanol.*" When I had made my *deposito*, she said, "I suggest that when you get to Chile you go to the teller with the name tag that says, 'I speak English.'"

I went to a Mexican restaurant and announced, "*Buenos dias. Cómo estás? Estoy aquí para el almuerzo.*" My waiter replied, "If you really feel a need to practice your Spanish, I'll get Maria."

In a blog titled "What Chile is Really Like," a tourist wrote, "Don't even think about trying your high school Spanish. They speak way too fast in a language no one teaches. They smile as though you are a first grader who has wandered into Calculus."

I have been in Chile three weeks and am sure of two things: 1) Any book with "Spanish" and "Easy" in the title was written by someone who has not been to Chile, and 2) Johnny Spanish is a liar.

On our first night a police officer said something that might have been, "It's really cold. Isn't it?" so I responded, "*Sí.*" I realized later that if he had asked, "Are you the bank robber we're looking for?" my answer would have been a poor choice.

I ordered in Spanish at a Starbucks and was given something I didn't recognize. Aren't *grande* and *venti* Italian? I got it wrong using three languages.

I was surprised at how many streets are named *Marcha Lento* until I learned this means "Slow down."

We went to the cinema and tried to ask what movie would be in English. The ticket salesperson two cash registers away delightedly asked, "May I help you?" Those are the only four English words she knows. And "750" sounded expensive until I realized that was when the movie started. We saw *Jersey Boys* with Spanish subtitles. It is not a good movie, but we now know several Spanish profanities.

I listened to a six-piece band on a street corner. When they got to the end, everyone sang along. I wrote down *Olvidado el relleno* and looked it up when I got home. I am still unclear why they were singing "I forgot the filling."

We found a place with "iced tea" on the menu (full disclosure—it is an Applebee's). I tried to order sweet tea and ended up with vanilla tea, which is not what we drink in Atlanta. And I must have said "no ice" without realizing it.

When asking for an item at the grocery store, I was excited to be given directions. Then I realized that they had sent us to the information booth. I could not figure out how to ask for salad dressing. My "*salsa para ensalada*" was not recognizable to the information specialist. Then I remembered something Johnny Spanish taught me and tried "*vestida para ensalada.*" She did not seem to know what a "salad dress" might be. Good luck with attempting to act out contact lens solution.

When Carol and I got in line, I quietly asked the cashier, "What is a good tip for the young man putting our four items into a bag?" She answered, "One hundred pesos," but Carol had already made the bag boy delirious with a tip considerably larger.

Here are the phrases I'm working on now:

- *Mi español es malo.* (My Spanish is bad.)
- *No entiendo.* (I don't understand.)
- *Por favor habla despacio.* (Please speak slowly.)
- *Me lo puede repetir?* (Could you repeat that?)
- *Sólo voy a estar hablando en tiempo presente.* (I will only be speaking in present tense.)

We went to a worship service at the Catedral Metropolitana de Santiago that was entirely in Spanish. The music was wonderful. I did not know many of the words, but something holy was happening. Some ways of communicating are beyond words.

When Jesus was blessing the meek, poor, and those who mourn, he may have considered, "*Felices son los estúpidos, porque aprenderan la humildad*" (Blessed are the stupid, for they will learn humility). Learning to measure myself and others by something more than the words we choose might be worth the trip.

Here's to God! (September 18, 2014)

During the second Skype interview with the church in Chile that I am now serving as interim pastor while on sabbatical, Arina, a lovely woman from Holland said, "We don't know many Baptists, so we need to ask three Baptist questions. The first is, 'How do you feel about communion twice a month?'"

I said, "That sounds great. The table is central to worship."

Arina seemed suspicious. "Okay, second question. What do you think about infant baptism?"

I said, "Throughout church history, most Christians have practiced infant baptism. It's a beautiful picture of God's love."

Arina said, "Alright, I guess. The third question is the hardest. The culture in Chile is different from yours. We have wine at church socials. Is that going to be a problem?"

I said, "I'm not sure what kind of Baptists you've met, but we're the other kind."

But now I am not so sure I am really the other kind.

I knew it was coming, but it was disconcerting. On Saturday night the church had an international dinner. Ninety of us—eighty-five of which qualify as international—gathered for appetizers from the Middle East, meat and potatoes from the Netherlands, and desserts from Argentina. On a given Sunday we are likely to have worshipers from Australia, Canada, England, Finland, Germany, Indonesia, Japan, New Zealand, Peru, South Africa, and Uruguay.

Our new congregation had Heineken in the serving line and two bottles of wine at every table.

As the meal began, I said, "This is the first time that I've been to a meal in a church fellowship hall where wine was served."

The Sunday school teachers, church council members, and ushers at my table were incredulous. They were as shocked as if I had said, "This is the first time I've been to a meal in a church fellowship hall without crack cocaine."

They were stunned: "What do you mean?"

"I've been to thousands of church suppers," I said, "and we've never had beer or wine."

"You're joking. Are you serious?" They were stupefied.

I said, "I wish I was joking, but the churches I've been part of have been serious about not serving alcohol at church."

I tried to explain Baptists, prohibition, and the dangers of alcoholism, but I did not get far. I was a Church of Christ minister explaining to Mozart why we do not like pianos. I was a Mormon bishop telling Dr Pepper how bad caffeine is. I was a Jewish rabbi attempting to help Jimmy Dean see the wisdom of not eating sausage.

The members of my new church were thrown by the sheer ludicrousness of the arguments I was offering, but they recovered enough to state the obvious. "Jesus turned water into wine. Don't your people think he knew what he was doing?"

"He gave the disciples wine at the Lord's Supper, but your churches serve a children's drink. Don't you think grape juice is horrible?"

Here's what I didn't say: I grew up in churches where it was important to identify sinners. In order to be the good people, we needed to recognize the bad people, so we decided what was sinful and what was OK. Drinking, smoking, and cussing were bad. Materialism, militarism, and homophobia were fine.

You could park in the church lot with a gun rack on your pick-up without questions, but if someone saw a Budweiser in your fridge, you would be the subject of conversation. Our church covenant included the promise "to abstain from the sale of, and use of, intoxicating drinks as a beverage," but did not have a word about the racism that surrounded us. I remember a sermon calling us to shop at Piggly Wiggly rather than Jitney Jungle because Piggly Wiggly did not sell beer, but I do not recall anything about the sexism that denied women opportunities.

I did not have a drink of wine until I was thirty years of age—at an Episcopal communion service—because the need to feel superior had been so ingrained in me.

At the end of a delightful meal, the church treasurer said, "You must go home and tell your Baptist friends how much fun we have. Take a bottle of wine to your next church fellowship."

I do not think this is the evangelism to which God calls me, but I might raise a glass to the kingdom bigger than I was taught.

Lost in the wilds of South America (October 17, 2014)

One way to explore a new city is to take a wrong turn, get lost, and discover new places by trying to figure out how to get back to the one place you know. This is something Carol and I tried shortly after getting to Santiago. Our experience was complicated by several factors.

I have no sense of direction—*nada, ninguno, cero.*

A few days after arriving in this city of six million, I went to several convenience stores, a metro stop, and a tourism center (!) asking for a map only to be told, "*No. Es difícil.*"

The GPS on my phone does not work south of Florida.

I do not see well enough to read the tiny letters on the tiny street signs that show up at random intersections.

It was late at night. It was not late when we got lost, but I understand now why elderly people do not drive at night.

We were in a country where we speak only a few words of the language and recognize even fewer. For instance, to an uneducated ear listening to high speed Chilean Spanish, "*derecho*" (right) sounds a lot like "*recto*" (straight ahead). I do know "*Estoy perdido*" (I am lost), which I used repeatedly.

The people we asked for directions were more amused by my poor Spanish than distressed at our predicament.

I stopped at a Walmart where the parking lot attendant found it hard to believe that anyone could get where we were while wanting to be where we wanted to be.

A woman taking out her trash was certain it was at least sixty kilometers, which sounds pretty far, to our house.

I tried to ask a street juggler at a busy intersection for directions, but he refused to break character. He seemed to think I was disparaging his art.

I stopped at an outdoor café where a young woman thought, "*¿Me puedes ayudar? Yo quiero ir a casa*" (Can you help me? I want to go home) was the worst pickup line she had ever heard.

We live two blocks from the tallest building in South America. You might think this would make it easy to get home, but our lighthouse turns out the lights when it is dark.

Chile feels no need to note the direction of the highway on which you are traveling. For instance, I spent a significant amount of time assuming that Costanera Norte went north and that if you were going the other direction it would be Costanera Sur, but this is not the case. (I have begun to suspect confusing signage is a clever way to encourage public transportation.)

Streets change names every few blocks for no discernible reason.

There are two roads named Americo Vespucio. One of them does not go where we needed to go.

One of the streets I most needed, La Avenida Libertador General Bernardo O'Higgins, is always called Alameda because who wants to keep saying La Avenida Libertador General Bernardo O'Higgins? It is still unclear why someone from Atlanta should be expected to know this.

We came really close to looking for a taxi and paying to follow them.

We eventually got home, but I have been lost frequently enough in the last three months to have time to reflect on this experience. A variety of religious faiths use the journey home as a metaphor for salvation. Jesus talked more about people being "lost" than being "sinners." The language of lostness is worth reclaiming if we recognize the despair of getting lost and the joy of finding our way home.

Missions and misconceptions (August 22, 2014)

When I was growing up in Mississippi, we sang, "We've a story to tell to the nations that shall turn their hearts to the right." We had to go so "the darkness shall turn to dawning, and the dawning to noonday bright." People all over the world were waiting for Southern Baptists to come so "Christ's great kingdom shall come on earth."

Missionaries went to distant lands (any country other than the United States) to encourage native women to wear shirts and pagan men not to eat missionaries. Their primary responsibility was to recite the Four Spiritual Laws and lead the foreigners in the sinners' prayer—which must be in the Bible somewhere.

These superstars came back from the mission field to show slides on Sunday nights: "This is the market where we bought goat brains—which tastes better than it sounds"; "This is the stream in which we beat our clothes against the rock"; "This is the hut where the chief and his seven wives live."

They told heartbreaking stories about children who have never made a Galilean village out of Popsicle sticks. They have never sung "Zacchaeus was a wee little man." They do not know the motions to "Deep and Wide."

We were the world's only hope.

Carol and I finally made it to the mission field. We are 4,700 miles from home serving a congregation with twenty nationalities, eighteen denominations, a few six-day creationists, and an atheist who comes because he likes the company.

Santiago Community Church in Santiago, Chile, does missions. The congregation cares for disabled adults and abandoned girls. The church includes people who would not find a place in many churches. Worship is sacred and joyful. Bible study is lively and thoughtful. And, get this: our church in Chile has offering envelopes, but they do not have a line on which to write your name. I am used to getting credit when I give money—and a tax break.

Carol and I attended a Catholic service in Spanish in a cathedral that was constructed in 1800 (before there were Southern Baptists). We didn't understand everything, but we recognized "Stand Up, Stand Up for Jesus"—which was not written by a Baptist—*Estad por Cristo firmes*.

We recited the Nicene Creed—written 1,300 years before Baptists existed—*Dios de Dios y Luz de Luz, Muy Dios de Muy Dios*. We prayed the Lord's Prayer, *Padre nuestro que estás en los cielos*. We shared the Lord's Supper, *Este es el cuerpo de Cristo*. Worship is filled with hope. The people are filled with Christ.

I was taught that we need to take Jesus to people who were not blessed by God to be born where we were born, but when I got here, I learned they have been worshiping Christ for a long time. They are already following Jesus—many more closely than I am.

We interpret the gospel through the lens of our environment. Churches make assumptions that are not shared by churches in other cultures. Sometimes the individualism in the United States leads to a "just me and Jesus" faith that neglects community. The Chilean people have an amazing commitment to friends and family. For many people in the United States, church functions as a break from their weekday jobs. In the church I am serving, jobs function for many as a way to live out their faith.

When we tailor the gospel to fit our desires, we end up with a partial gospel. Chileans cannot understand how a "Christian" country could sell handguns at Walmart, a wealthy "Christian" country could allow so many to be homeless, and a "Christian" country could support capital punishment or spend more than half of its discretionary government funding on military purposes.

Maybe sharing the gospel is just that—sharing the gospel and exploring the gospel that is bigger than any country. I will go home to Atlanta with a bigger vision of God and a greater concern for the world.

We have a story to tell to the nations, but the nations have a lot of stories we need to hear. We cannot take God anywhere without discovering that God was there long before we arrived. Missions is the opportunity to listen, learn, and share "the kingdom of love and light."

A Chilean love story: A Catholic priest and his wife (November 21, 2014)

Joseph came to Santiago, Chile, in 1974 as the new priest at a two-priest parish. Early each morning and late each evening a young woman walked past his window. After several months, he asked where she was going.

Isabel said, "My brother is being held a few blocks from here. If I go every day, they may be less likely to kill him. They need to know that someone cares."

When Joseph learned that she was traveling two hours each way, he said, "You should stay here."

She did secretarial work a few hours a week to feel better about accepting their help. When her brother was executed, the church offered her a full-time job.

The kind priest became her boss. They loved the church and enjoyed each other's company.

After a few years Isabel confessed to Brian, the second priest, "I'm in love with Joseph."

Brian answered like he was supposed to, "Never say that again. Joseph has made a vow to God."

She did not say anything.

A few months passed before Joseph confessed to Brian, "I'm in love with Isabel."

Brian said, "Never say that again. You've made a vow to God."

Joseph and Isabel did not tell one another how they felt for 15 years. Then, on a visit with his mother in the United States, something changed. Joseph decided that God approved, even if the church did not. He called Isabel in Chile and began with, "Will you marry me?"

They had never been on a date, shared a kiss, or confessed their love. She said, "Yes."

They had a civil wedding and immediately lost their jobs and the places they lived. Their savings were held by the church—which was not happy with them.

They admitted to a landlord that they had no money, and he said, "I love your story. The first three months are free."

Isabel became pregnant. The doctor said, "I love your story. I'll take care of your baby for free."

Joseph got a job. They continued to petition for a church wedding. The religious bureaucrats sent Joseph a form that included the statement that when he took his vows he was mistaken. Joseph knew it was not true. He had been a good priest for fifteen years. He would not sign it.

The church did not relent for eleven years. When their marriage was finally allowed, Joseph and Isabel asked Brian, who was still their friend, to perform the ceremony. Their ten-year-old daughter Elizabeth cried through the wedding.

I met Joseph at the funeral of a 90-year-old woman who loved Joseph and Isabel. Joseph told the congregation how the woman pretended to be serious though she loved to laugh. He suggested the woman was so kind, her last words could have been, "Make sure you thank the doctors. They did their best."

I rode from the church to the cemetery with the woman's three daughters. They talked about how Joseph continued to be their mother's priest after the church told him he was not a priest, how he cared for their mother after their father died, and how he visited as her health failed. They asked me not to share his real name—which I have changed—because he wouldn't be comfortable with the attention.

At the cemetery I tried to get Joseph to tell me more: "During the funeral you spoke like someone who has spoken in church before."

He answered, "I've been there and done that."

Joseph looks like Clint Eastwood. Isabel is a Chilean Yoko Ono. The most amazing part of these weathered saints' story is that they are still devoted to the church.

The next time I am in a conversation about ordination I will think of them. Joseph must have been a great priest, but he may be an even better ex-priest. God's ordination and the church's may not have much in common.

The next time I am in a hurry I will think of them—fifteen years of waiting, eleven years of waiting. I want everything now, but God's saints live with patience.

The next time I want to complain about the church I will think of them. Some days the church shows little kindness, but if Joseph and Isabel can continue to love the church, I can, too.

Your world is too small (January 23, 2015)

Less than ten percent of the world's population speaks English as their primary language. Less than five percent of the world lives in the United States. Less than two percent of the world is Baptist. Less than 1/100 of 1 percent of the world is a member of a Cooperative Baptist Fellowship church. I have spent most of my life in a good but tiny corner of the world.

A Malaysian saying argues that too many live with limited vision, "like frogs under coconut shells." Perhaps if, as J.B. Philips put it, "Your God is too small," it is because our world is too small. St. Augustine wrote, "The world is a book and those who do not travel read only a page."

Six months ago, Carol and I went where 99 percent of the population is happy to speak Spanish in a country that is not the United States. While serving as the interim pastor of Santiago Community Church, during a party at the manse (Anglican for parsonage), I said, "Carol is the only Baptist I have seen in several months."

A Taiwanese woman, Sophia, replied, "I'm a Baptist."

Sophia and Carol are the only Baptists I saw for several months. The church we served was made up of people from twenty-three nationalities and eighteen denominations.

Carol and I hiked along the Pacific and in the Andes. We saw sea lions, penguins, and a blow hole. We ate pepinos, pastel de choclo, and Super Ocho candy bars.

We celebrated Chilean Independence Week and the country's newest holiday, "Protestant Day." We were entertained by the Andes Highlanders dance team and a jazz tango trio. At a Muslim Iftar I met a diplomat from Iraq whose wife left him in Paris—which he does not consider the most romantic city in the world.

Carol and I went salsa dancing, horseback riding, and to the fifty-sixth anniversary of a fire station that has a swimming pool. We saw the world's largest swimming pool. I visited two of Pablo Neruda's three houses and read two-thirds of a book of his poetry without understanding why he won the Nobel Prize.

We enjoyed being in a country with pictures of Nobel Prize winning poets (Gabriela Mistral) on their money instead of Indian fighters (Andrew Jackson). I was, for the first time, mistaken for an Australian. When asked to bring something exotic from her home country, Carol took Dr Pepper.

We drank coffee with the Archbishop of Canterbury and learned to greet people with a holy kiss just like Paul said we should. We shared church with people who climbed Kilimanjaro, ran with the bulls of Pamplona, and hitchhiked to South America from Wisconsin. I led a Bible study that included a twenty-seven-year-old who has been to forty-one countries and bull-riding camp. I worshiped with people who were shocked to meet someone who has lived in only one country.

We shared church with courageous people who became Christians as adults and had their lives changed. God reinvented them.

My experience is that people who have seen the world tend to have a bigger view of God. People who know only those like themselves begin to think God is like them.

Thomas Aquinas said, "I have seen things that make my writings like straw."

Most preachers do not have to see much for that to be true for their preaching, so seeing the world helps. The more we understand how big God's world is, the more we recognize that some things we ignore matter and some things we give a lot of attention to do not. When I studied the Pentecost story (different nations coming together in the Spirit) with young adults from Chile, Finland, Germany, El Salvador, New Zealand, the Netherlands, and Jamaica, I was reminded that the church belongs to a Spirit that is bigger than we realize.

Ministers are tempted to focus on the success of the institution, but the world needs God. We need to preach to ultimate concerns—love, joy, and peace. Churches need to speak of God, who is bigger than we have been led to believe.

The kingdom of God does not extend as far as we can see. The kingdom is far bigger. When the trumpet sounds for the party to end all parties, we are not going to recognize many of the people there. Come that great homecoming parade, the processional will be filled with those who have nothing in common but the grace of God that invites us home.

Life in Brooklyn

A Southerner living in a foreign land—Brooklyn (June 9, 2016)

"Yankee" was a term of derision in my fourth grade class.

When the teacher announced, "We have a new student who just moved to Mississippi from New York," we looked on his poor little lost soul with pity.

The progressive ten-year-olds argued, "It's not his fault he's from New York."

Each year on the Wednesday night before the Home Mission Offering, the director of missions would display a map of the United States with red dots representing churches. The southern states were completely red, but the northern states looked like they had mild cases of chicken pox.

"We have to get missionaries to these unchurched people," he pleaded.

I was fifteen before I realized that the red dots did not represent all churches but only Southern Baptist churches. That seems like a detail worth mentioning.

I was taught that the South had cornered the market on Jesus, morality, friendliness, food, and football.

I recently moved from Atlanta to Brooklyn, from a beloved home to a foreign land.

New York is a different world.

I drank an egg cream—which contains neither egg nor cream.

The walk/don't walk signs are just suggestions.

Pumping your own gas is illegal across the river in New Jersey.

I have not taken my car out of the parking garage since we arrived.

If you put outgoing mail in your mailbox, it will stay there.

The baby strollers cost more than my car—and have more features.

On those rare occasions that sweet tea appears on a menu, it is a lie.

Chain stores are notable for their absence. Bookstores, coffee shops, and beer makers are home-grown and independent. Empire Mayonnaise, for instance, only sells artisanal mayonnaise. I can't see this catching on in Alabama.

The Brooklyn Dodgers—who left for Los Angeles in 1957—are still some people's favorite baseball team.

Soccer and lacrosse are considered sports.

Some of Brooklyn looks like *Brooklyn Nine-Nine*, but most, not so much.

Henry Ward Beecher, famous abolitionist,
welcomes the Youngers to Brooklyn

I have not heard any of these: "dese," "dem," "dose," "youse guys," or "fuhgeddaboudit."

The neighbors brought bread and a list of good grocery stores. People who live this close together need to get along.

The bagels here are better. The hot dogs are not.

A four-story, eight-room house is like living on a Stairmaster.

A stoop is a porch without rocking chairs.

Hipsters are nice people trying too hard not to impress us.

Natives of Brooklyn have also been lied to. People keep offering grits—which I have eaten exactly once in my life.

A couple of days ago, someone on the street asked me for directions. Apparently, tourists don't know who to ask.

Our new church thinks "Northern hospitality" should be a phrase. Our fridge and pantry were stocked when we arrived. A crew showed up on Memorial Day to unpack "Atlanta Peach Moving" boxes. We enjoyed a different cook's offerings each night for the first week—nothing fried. Our first Sunday was lots of fun. The banner hanging on Henry Ward Beecher's statue said, "Welcome Youngers," but it felt like "Welcome Home."

My parents think Carol and I have gone to the mission field, but we are sharing church with people who have their own joyful ways of sharing church.

I love my Southern heritage. The churches of my childhood included good people who loved Jesus and taught me to do the same. I will miss college football, driving a car, and having a yard that requires more than a pair of scissors to mow. But I am discovering again what we all know but tend to forget. The gospel is bigger than any region, any country, and any one understanding of the gospel.

When the search committee announced, "We have a new minister who just moved to New York from Georgia," I am sure some looked with pity on what they thought of as my poor little lost soul, but by the grace of God we can learn from each other.

Still learning to see the third time across the Brooklyn Bridge (July 7, 2016)

Brett Younger, New Yorker

I like running to Manhattan, and I love running back to Brooklyn—though *running* may not be the right word. I have trotted across the Brooklyn Bridge three times. I go slow enough not to miss much.

According to an unreliable source, more than 4,000 pedestrians and 2,000 bicyclists cross the bridge each day. No one is counting the scooters, skaters, and skateboarders. The great majority are not from around here.

The parents wear Yankees caps they bought fifteen minutes earlier. The children wear foam Statue of Liberty headdresses. They debate the merits of a New York key ring versus a New York key chain—which I am pretty sure are the same thing. They gawk, gaze, and ogle. Their eyes are wide. Their jaws are slack.

My third trip across the bridge was on July 4th. For the first time I reacted like many real New Yorkers. I was annoyed.

The lanes are clearly marked. Distracted pedestrians to the left, racing bicycles to the right, and sluggish joggers on the line that divides them. There is room for three people to walk side by side, so tourists tend to spread out in groups of six. This puts the slow-moving runners on a collision course with the fast-moving bicyclists.

Tourists take lots of pictures. The selfies are bad enough, but the selfie sticks are infuriating. These monopods allow the photographers and their enraptured subjects to be six feet apart and send everyone into the high-speed lane.

When I pass a shutterbug, I wave. I am part of several Iowans' photo albums of their trip to New York. These omnipresent tourists make you understand why New Yorkers keep selling the bridge to them.

I want to say, "If you want a New York experience, don't rent a pedicab, get in line at Grimaldi's, or buy an Empire State Building mug. Walk to Cranberry's, get a bagel, and read *The New York Times*."

I am at my most annoyed when, a block from home, a family from the Czech Republic has their smiling seven-year-old—whose English must be the strongest—ask, "Where to walk Brooklyn Bridge?"

I am jealous. They are more excited about the bridge than I am.

Here is the problem. On your third trip across the Brooklyn Bridge you might not notice how many love-struck couples write the date and their initials on a padlock, latch it on to a cable, and throw the key in the East River. This romantic act represents the love that will last until the city sends workers to cut the locks off.

On your third trip across the bridge you may cease to be curious about the bridge on which you saunter. If you don't read the historical marker the first time you may never read it. You might not notice that the bridge is 133 years old. At the opening, they had a band, fireworks, and President Chester Arthur. The bridge cost $15 million. Twenty-seven people died during its construction.

On your third trip across the bridge you might not even care that early on there were rumors the bridge was going to collapse, so P.T. Barnum led a parade of twenty-one elephants over the bridge, or that they used to store wine under the Manhattan end because it was easy to keep at sixty degrees.

What if I stop being amazed by this amazing bridge? I live in the greatest city in the world. What if I start taking it for granted? What if I stop hearing the multiplicity of languages? What if I cease to be astonished by the ethnic restaurants? What if I stop noticing the Statue of Liberty?

I want to be a tourist—wide-eyed, slack-jawed, and surprised. People come all over the world to visit my hometown because New York is busy and beautiful and something astounding is going on all of the time.

My hometown has coffee places not named Starbucks, bookstores not named Barnes and Noble, and pizza places not named Domino's. We have neighborhoods that do not look like the next neighborhood. I want to feel surprise when I see dogs in baby strollers and feel peace when I sit on my stoop. I want to be a sightseer.

We get so used to the extraordinary that we stop seeing.

To be a person of faith is to be a tourist. In some ways, the longer Christians work at the business of being Christians, the more difficult it is. We are dulled by our familiarity with what we have been given. We do not feel the excitement a visitor feels.

When the community of Jesus' followers acts the way Christ dreamed we would, there is nothing like it. We pay attention to those around us. We listen carefully, speak kindly, and overcome differences. We find grace in welcoming strangers. We are amazed.

I plan to keep running on the Brooklyn Bridge, so the tourists can teach me to see.

Abraham Lincoln, Susan B. Anthony, and Adam Sandler: Signs of a church that is more than a museum (September 1, 2016)

Years ago, when attendance was low, Plymouth Church in Brooklyn, New York, brought in a consultant who said, "You can either be a museum or a church."

The consultant had been going to the wrong museums. A good church is like a good children's museum—a place to learn, explore, and discover.

On the tripadvisor.com list of things to do in Brooklyn, Plymouth Church is No. 82—behind the Coney Island Museum, but ahead of the Coney Island Brewing Company.

I have interrupted five groups of tourists in front of the church for no good reason. One tour guide suggested I point out any mistakes he made—and soon regretted it. I caught a mistake on another tour, but the guide was speaking Spanish, so I let it go.

They miss some details, but the guides are good at fitting the tour to whichever tourists paid the thirty bucks. When the tour was filled with teenagers, the guide talked about Adam Sandler making a movie at our church. (*The Cobbler* suffers in comparison to earlier classics, such as *Happy Gilmore* and *The Waterboy*.)

When the tour was an African American choir, the guide described the Fisk University Choir singing in our sanctuary in 1871. The concert was so successful the choir sang at the White House shortly thereafter.

When the tour was a group of Jehovah's Witnesses, the guide completely skipped our church's role in the abolitionist movement, women's suffrage, and civil rights, but pointed to a house across the street where Charles Taze Russell's cousin lived. Who knew?

Left to right, Brett Younger, Henry Ward Beecher

Plymouth has an amazing history. When I sit in pew 89, I wonder what Abraham Lincoln prayed when he sat there. I have turned off the lights in the basement—where slaves escaping to freedom passed through the Underground Railroad—and imagined what it feels like to run for your life. When I am in my office, I often think of Branch Rickey—a member of Plymouth Church and general manager of the Brooklyn Dodgers—praying there until he decided that God wanted him to invite Jackie Robinson to integrate baseball.

Some of our church's heritage is complicated. The sculptor of a statue of Henry Ward Beecher and a bas-relief of Abraham Lincoln in our church garden was Gutzon Borglum, who also created Mount Rushmore. Borglum was a member of the Klan.

Beecher, the founding pastor, was a gifted minister who fought courageously against slavery and was considered the most famous man in America. His adultery trial sold a lot of newspapers and ended in a hung jury.

The portrait of Henry Ward Beecher in our arcade does not make him look particularly attractive. Mark Twain wrote, "Mr. Beecher is a remarkably handsome man when he is in the full tide of sermonizing, and his face is lit up with animation, but he is as homely as a singed cat when he isn't doing anything."

The list of people who have been in our building is surprising—Ralph Waldo Emerson, Frederick Douglass, Susan B. Anthony, Harriet Beecher Stowe, Hillary Clinton, Sonia Sotomayor, Elliott Spitzer, Colin Kaepernick, Norah Jones, and Adam Driver.

A couple of years ago, one of our committees was asked to name the three biggest moments in the church's history. They picked Henry Ward Beecher's tenure as the first pastor, Martin Luther King Jr. preaching an early version of his "I Have a Dream" sermon at Plymouth, and the church recommitting itself to Jesus Christ in 2004. Plymouth's resurgence is part of the story.

Every church has a history. Churches stuck in their history keep talking about how great it once was. Churches that have forgotten their history mistakenly believe that there are no good gifts older than they are.

We can be grateful for our past without being trapped in it. We do not need to choose between being a museum and a church. We explore what God has done and discover that God is still at work.

Why New York needs churches (October 27, 2016)

When my stylist at Supercuts finds out that I have only lived in Brooklyn for five months, she offers to explain New York to me. She looks me in the eye and says, "If you love New York, she will love you back. If you don't love New York, then you need to leave right now."

I love New York, and most days she loves me back. I am at a conference with ministers from around the country at Riverside Church in Manhattan. When asked, "Where are you from?" I answer, "Brooklyn," and a friend from North Carolina laughs. I smile, but it hurts my feelings. I may not sound like I am from Brooklyn, but this is my home.

I wake up in the morning and thank God that I am here. The river, the skyline, and the people rushing around make me grateful. I am thankful for the amazing art, theater, and food. Our city is vibrant, diverse, and resilient.

A lady waiting in line tells me, "My neighbor moved to Oregon. How could she do that? Why would anyone leave New York to move to Oregon? I thought she was smart, but I was wrong."

I know enough to reply, "She's going to regret it."

But I have also been here long enough to know that New York is complicated. I get in line at Cranberry's for my regular iced coffee and a chocolate croissant—the breakfast of champions. The woman in front of me orders in Spanish. I think, "I can do that"—"*Quiero una gran café con leche y azúcar y un croissant de chocolate.*" I am a member of Cranberry's "Buy ten cups of coffee and get one large free!" club. This is a promotion for people whose math skills are so deficient they believe this deal warrants an exclamation point. I am, nonetheless, enough of a regular to be well on my way to a second free iced coffee. I secretly figure I have been here enough for the cashier to give me what I always order even if I say it wrong. She compliments my Spanish. I previously considered her an honest person. She hands me a chocolate croissant and a hot coffee. Apparently, I do not know the Spanish word for ice. I am still living in a foreign country.

Some things are more difficult in New York. Driving unpainted, narrow streets filled with bicycles, scooters, adventurous pedestrians, and aggressive taxi drivers is frightening. Parking—alternate side unless it is a street-cleaning weekday with an R in it 8 a.m. to 6 p.m.—is confusing. Paying a reasonable amount for housing is impossible. Raising a family is tough. Helping children get the best education is complicated. Lugging groceries home is problematic. Finding a quiet place or a restroom or a way to retire is tricky. Being kind is challenging. Making friends is difficult. Feeling like you matter is hard.

New York makes it clear that we need the church. We need a space in the midst of the secular to remember the holy. We need others to help us recognize God's presence. When the city treats us poorly and we feel confused, alone, or sad, we need a family.

We need a church because we need a place where people know who we are, treat us with kindness, and let us be kind. We need a place where people listen to us, talk about things that matter, and trust us. We need a place to spend time with children and senior adults, be around those with a deep sense of spirituality, and serve those who need our help. We need a place to pray, sing, give, and listen for the Spirit. We need Jesus. We need Christ's church.

Dorothy Parker said, "London is satisfied, Paris is resigned, but New York is always hopeful. Always it believes that something good is about to come off, and it must hurry to meet it."

That is a good description of the church New Yorkers need—always hopeful, believing something good is about to happen, hurrying to meet God.

Underground church business meetings—and God actually shows up (March 13, 2017)

Try to imagine the church business meetings that made this happen. During the early 1800s, the network of churches and individuals helping those escaping slavery was known as the Underground Railroad. My congregation, Plymouth Church in Brooklyn, New York, was "the Grand Central Depot of the Underground Railroad." We give tours of the church basement where runaway slaves hid. The guides turn out the lights and tell visitors to "imagine hiding in the dark, hearing someone coming down those stairs, and praying they can't hear your heart pound."

As far as I know, none of our tour guides tell visitors to "imagine the church business meeting where they argued about whether to help these people," but the business meeting is equally amazing and easier to imagine.

"Why can't the church stay out of politics? This is a partisan issue. We want people from both sides of the aisle to feel welcome in our congregation. Some of our biggest givers aren't going to like this."

"How do we know the people we're helping aren't dangerous? They could harm somebody. What if one of our girls gets hurt? Who wants to be responsible for that?"

"What's the vetting process? Normal vetting isn't enough. We need extreme vetting."

"Churches shouldn't be breaking the law. Our ministers need to set a good example. If people want to change the situation, they can write letters to Congress. There's another election in four years."

"Don't we have enough to do taking care of ourselves? We have a stove that needs repairing and a sidewalk that's a lawsuit waiting to happen. Why don't we focus on those things?"

At some point in a long contentious meeting, someone pointed out that Jesus and many of his followers were executed by the government. The leaders of the first church were in and out of jail. The early Christians believed that God's people have promised to do more than stay out of trouble.

The church business meeting where a congregation decides to take risks to help someone other than themselves is about as close as we get to proof of the existence of God.

Churches across the United States are having difficult conversations. Many are part of what they are calling the New Underground Railroad.

Recent executive orders on immigration and two Department of Homeland Security memos move past earlier guidelines to focus only on criminals for deportation and instead put undocumented immigrants at risk of deportation for something as minor as a traffic ticket. We are being asked to ignore the fact that immigrants are statistically much less likely to commit crimes than native-born Americans.

The present administration's ramping up deportations raises new questions, but the immigration system has not been compassionate or effective for a long time. We break families apart and penalize the kind of people we most need in our country. Since 1995 the United States has allowed 5,000 visas per year for unskilled workers—and a guest worker program of about 200,000. But for years this country has imported most of its agricultural workers, so twelve million people work in the shadows. Ninety percent of undocumented men are working because our country needs their labor.

People who do not think of themselves as political but who take their faith seriously feel compelled to do something. Churches are resisting the deportation of undocumented immigrants. They believe that the Jewish tradition compels us to practice hospitality to the foreigner. They recognize that the Gospels are clear about the Christian requirement to care for the outsider. Jesus warns those who pretend to follow, "I was a stranger and you did not welcome me."

The Sanctuary Movement includes more than 800 courageous congregations that have committed to protecting immigrants. They pledge to pray, educate, and give money. Churches have formed study groups that are looking for thoughtful, courageous ways to follow Christ's instructions. Churches are preparing to use private homes as part of a modern-day underground railroad to move undocumented immigrant families to Canada.

Churches are having business meetings and God is showing up.

Frankly speaking: An Independence Day showdown with drama, daring, and indigestion (July 6, 2018)

When you hear the words "American hero," you may think of Abraham Lincoln, Susan B. Anthony, or Martin Luther King Jr., but a lot of people think of Joey "Jaws" Chestnut. On July 4, 2018, the eyes of the world were on Coney Island, host to a gut-busting Independence Day showdown that provided drama, daring, and indigestion.

Two dear friends who relish this outlandish event promised it would be fun. We arrived an hour early but could not get close enough to smell the nitrates. The smell of America was, nonetheless, in the air. Thousands of us, many wearing wiener hats, gathered to cheer the dogfight for the mustard yellow belt emblematic of frankfurter-eating supremacy.

The Brooklyn Community Choir sang because someone thought gospel music would be a helpful addition to the festivities.

The announcer, George Shea, is a poet. Here is some notable commentary:

"His good cholesterol is low. His bad cholesterol is high. His BMI is borderline presidential."

"He stands before us like Hercules himself. Albeit a large, bald Hercules at an eating contest."

"This is like watching Picasso paint."

"When all the world's languages are poured into a single bowl, the word that unites us will be freedom." (I do not know what this means, but the crowd cheered ecstatically.)

Two non-contestants at Nathan's Hot Dog Eating Contest

Joey Chestnut, the pride of the red, white, and blue, claimed his eleventh Nathan's Hot Dog Eating Contest title. (LeBron James has only won three NBA titles.) Joey inhaled a staggering seventy-four hot dogs in ten minutes—a little less than one every eight seconds. In this stupefying act, Joey consumed 22,000 calories and 1,332 grams of fat. The carb count stirred the hearts of patriots: 1,776 carbs. That's right—1776! (This statistic should ensure Joey's invitation to the White House.) As the crowd chanted "USA," this gustatory gladiator processed more beef than a slaughterhouse. The lesser competitors suffered reversals, which are exactly what they sound like.

The fine art of oinking out is governed by Major League Eating, which also handles crab cakes, baked beans, butter—just butter—and cow brains. As would be expected when there is a $10,000 prize, there have been accusations of performance enhancing drugs. Some claim that Joey lines his intestines with aloe. Other gurgitators—including Takeru Kobayashi, the legend who is no longer welcome at Coney Island—have been accused of having their stomachs surgically altered. The gastronomic gamesmanship of Nathan's Famous chow-down is, for many, a celebration of what makes America great.

I love an extravaganza that makes you never want to eat again as much as the next person, but this festival of belching and burping raises questions. Is overindulgence a feat to be celebrated? Should binging be considered a sport? What is the over/under on the date of Joey's death? Why is he still alive? Should anyone eat seventy-four hot dogs in ten minutes while children starve? (Carol asked this several times, but the good and clever people at Nathan's make a point of donating 100,000 hot dogs to the Food Bank of New York City each July 4.) Should a cardiologist be doing the play-by-play? Should Pepto-Bismol be a sponsor? Would this be more appropriate on the Food Network than ESPN? What kind of parents raise their child to compete in a gorge-a-thon?

Gluttony seems particularly unattractive when it is televised. We cheer for the wrong things. Our society gives itself to wretched excess. Our insatiable appetite leaves us without an appreciation for what is truly good.

I am still dealing with my feelings about what I witnessed. For lunch today, I had a salad.

Before I die . . . (February 18, 2016)

When the waitress brought our food, I tried to find a way to ask, "How am I supposed to eat this?"

I had to think fast.

I came up with, "How am I supposed to eat this?"

She explained with kindness and condescension, "You can eat it however you want, but I suggest you pour this over the rice. Dip the bread in this sauce. This is the dessert so don't pour anything on it."

Carol and I were having dinner in Decatur, Georgia, with August, whom we met in Santiago, Chile. I first suggested Farm Burger, but that choice did not seem adventurous to Carol, so we tried to be more interesting and went for Indian street food. This was a move in the right direction for August, but it takes a lot to register on his interesting meter. August has climbed Mount Kilimanjaro and run with the bulls of Pamplona.

He speaks three languages. He has been to bull-riding camp and rafted on the Amazon. He bungee-jumped in Brazil and skydived in Norway. When people make bucket lists, their lists would look like August's Christmas letter if he had a Christmas letter—which he does not because he is too interesting for that.

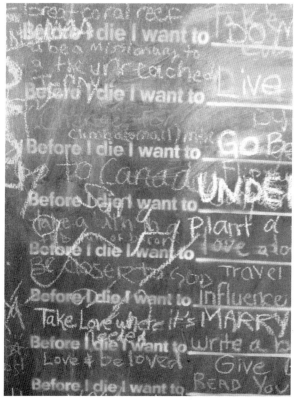

A Community Bucket List

When you have dinner with August, the temptation is to think your life is dull. I am not sure what countries Kilimanjaro (Rwanda?) and Pamplona (Spain?) are in. My Spanish makes people who speak Spanish roll their eyes. I do not want to ride a bull or a raft. I have an overwhelming desire to stay in the plane.

Our list is not as impressive as August's, but Carol and I have done a few things that show up on bucket lists. We have been to Paris, Amsterdam, and London. We took a train to Oxford to sit in C.S. Lewis's pew. We lived in South America where we hiked the Andes (with August) and had a cup of coffee with the Archbishop of Canterbury. We sang along with Jimmy Buffett and Bruce Springsteen, and we stood silently at Elvis' grave. We rode one rollercoaster together. We ate lunch in the booth where JFK proposed to Jackie, and we kept President Carter waiting while Carol talked to her mother on the phone.

Bucket lists took an artistic turn in 2011 when Candy Chang painted the side of an abandoned house in her New Orleans neighborhood. She had lost someone she loved and was dealing with depression when she used chalkboard paint and stenciled a grid with the sentence, "Before I die I want to _____." Anybody walking by could pick up a piece of chalk and share a dream.

By the next day, the wall was full of responses. Before I die I want to . . . Sing for millions. Plant a tree. Play the piano. Sail around the world. Swim without holding my nose. See my daughter graduate. Abandon all insecurities. Be a teacher. Eat more of everything.

Over one thousand "Before I Die" walls have been created in more than thirty-five languages and in more than seventy countries. I stood in front of the wall in Asheville, North Carolina, and thought about the people whose goal before they die is to . . . Swim in a pool of golden retriever puppies. Go to India. Do a cartwheel. Make it in hip hop. Go to a World Series game at Wrigley Field. Straddle the international dateline. Trace their roots back to Italy. Fall in love. Proudly wear a bikini. Win an Oscar. Own a llama farm.

Some are heartbreaking. Before I die I want to . . . Hold her one more time. Find a cure for my daughter's disease. Make my dad proud again.

But most of us could do better. Being a great salsa dancer is a fine goal, but we should aim higher. Before I die I want to . . . Tell good stories. Work for justice. Be the exception to a lousy rule. Give to feed starving children. Care for my family. Care for someone else's family. Forgive the one person I was not planning to forgive. Love someone enough to weep when they weep. Become more like Christ. Help a church become more like Christ. Show someone who has almost given up how to hope again.

Share our dreams.

The Year in Review for Thoughtful Christians (you might have missed something) (December 18, 2019)

You thought you were paying attention, but you may have missed a few things. While *CNN's Year in Review* will catch you up on the news stories, it will not tell you how thoughtful Christians responded to those stories. If you are a thoughtful Christian, then this is the year in review for you.

January 1

The Netflix series *Tidying Up with Marie Kondo* prescribed an order for moving through a household and deciding what to keep: clothes, books, papers, miscellaneous items, and sentimental items. This is the order for churches: ancient pageant costumes, old hymnals, business meeting minutes, untunable upright pianos, and church directories from the 1990s.

January 3

2019 started with a partial government shutdown. President Trump wanted $5.6 billion for a wall to keep refugees out. The Democrats gave him money for border security. The person wiping the tears off the Statue of Liberty worked without pay.

January 3

Pope Francis sent a letter to United States bishops pointing out that they handled the recent sex abuse scandals poorly. He said that blaming each other and covering up is not helpful. Some blamed the pope for blaming the bishops.

January 8

A report came out that the United States' carbon dioxide emissions in 2018 had the biggest increase in eight years. The US is getting literal heat for leaving the Paris climate agreement. Several church staff meetings included this conversation:

"We need to do something in worship about climate change. When is Earth Day?"

"It's the day after Easter."

"Maybe next year."

January 8
A report says that millions of Americans think they have food allergies, but they do not. The number of churches serving the "gluten-free body of Christ" continues to increase.

January 15
President Trump ordered piles of fast food for CFP National Champions, the Clemson Tigers, for their White House visit. On January 16, several churches served piles of fast food for Wednesday night supper and called it a "Church State Dinner."

January 15
The CBF Governing Board hired Paul Baxley, senior minister of First Baptist Church in Athens, Georgia, to succeed Executive Coordinator Suzii Paynter. Texans suddenly understood how Italians feel about a pope from Argentina.

January 16
Jilmar Ramos-Gomez was born in Grand Rapids and fought in Afghanistan, but the local sheriff's office turned him over to ICE. Conservative ministers continue looking for Bible verses opposing immigration, but they haven't found any yet.

January 23
A new report stated that Islam is on track to surpass Christianity as the world's biggest religion. This news led evangelicals to a greater appreciation for the Catholic approach to birth control.

January 28
After a *Fox & Friends* report that lawmakers in six states have introduced measures to permit public school children to study the Bible, unemployed seminary graduates who used to believe in the separation of church and state updated their resumes.

January 31
According to the Pew Research Center, religious people are more likely to exercise but are not more likely to have a healthy body mass index. Religious people exercise more and are fatter than regular people. Further research is needed on the effects of church picnics, sitting in pews, and how many church people lie about exercising.

February 12
A *San Antonio Express-News* and *Houston Chronicle* investigation reported that Southern Baptist Churches hired at least thirty-five ministers who faced sexual misconduct charges. Several Southern Baptist scholars have started writing, "What we should have learned from the Catholics."

February 22
Tim Tebow made *Run the Race*, "the Christian movie he always wanted to see." Sixty percent of the critics on Rotten Tomatoes said it was a Christian movie they did not want to see.

February 26
The United Methodist Church voted against allowing LGBT clergy and same-sex marriage. The "Traditional Plan" upholds and expands the church's 1972 stance that homosexuality is "incompatible with Christian teaching." The "Traditional Plan" does not mention the tradition of polygamy found throughout the Hebrew Scriptures.

March 1
For more than a decade, the interfaith group No More Deaths has been placing food, clothing, and water in the Sonoran Desert to help migrants who have crossed into Arizona from Mexico. They cite Jesus' command to give water to the thirsty. A federal judge found volunteers guilty of entering a national refuge without a permit and abandonment of property. He sentenced them to fifteen months of unsupervised probation and fined each $250. The judge did not mention Jesus during sentencing.

March 7
David Brooks's column "The Case for Reparations: A Slow Convert to the Cause" made many white people think seriously about their feelings for David Brooks.

March 11
Barbara Brown Taylor's *Holy Envy* called readers to a greater appreciation of world religions. Someone somewhere is working on *Holy Arrogance*, which calls readers to a greater appreciation of what they already thought.

March 11
Betsy DeVos, the education secretary, sent a letter to Congress indicating that she wants religious schools to be eligible for federal funding and grants. This clears the way for Americans who would never give money to Oral

Roberts, Bob Jones, or Brigham Young to contribute to Oral Roberts, Bob Jones, and Brigham Young.

March 13
Researchers warn that religious self-flagellation poses a cancer risk. Scientists argue, "It is likely that either sharing blood-stained blades, contact of infected blood with open wounds, or with infected medical equipment resulted in [a cancer-causing virus's] transmission." Some question whether those who practice self-flagellation are likely to read the report in the *Center for Disease Control and Prevention's Emerging Infectious Diseases Journal.*

March 18
After fifty people were killed in terror attacks in Christchurch, New Zealand, Prime Minister Jacinda Ardern declared, "Within ten days of this horrific act we will have announced reforms which will, I believe, make our community safer." She drew a comparison to Australia, which moved rapidly to enact strict gun laws after its own mass shooting in 1996. Lawmakers in the United States had no response because they were on spring break.

March 25
Michigan Attorney General Dana Nessel said discrimination in adoption services, even for religious objections, "is illegal, no matter the rationale." Discrimination in religious services continues to be legal, no matter how stupid the rationale.

March 26
North Dakota Governor Burgum lifted the ban on Sunday morning shopping. Under the old "blue laws," businesses could not open until noon. Ministers in North Dakota know blue laws are goofy but do not really need the competition from Target.

March 29
The San Antonio City Council voted to prevent Chick-fil-A from opening in the city's airport. The council did not like Chick-fil-A's donations to groups opposing same-sex marriage, but most voters in Texas love Chick-fil-A's Spicy Deluxe Sandwich and do not care for couples that are spicy in the wrong way. Youth ministers in San Antonio were disappointed that their chicken sandwiches were once again a question of faith.

April 4
The Church of Jesus Christ of Latter-day Saints repealed its 2015 ruling that banned baptisms for children of gay parents until they were eighteen. The religious world was shocked to learn that there are gay Mormon parents.

April 15
A disastrous fire broke out at the Notre Dame Cathedral, causing widespread damage. In the United States, church building and grounds committees added "check the fire extinguishers" to their agenda.

April 17
Mahavir Jayanti, the most important holiday for followers of Jainism, was observed in India. Lord Mahavira, the last of the twenty-four Jain deities, was born on April 17. Americans who disparage this holiday need to remember that in the United States, April 17 is—you can look this up—National Cheeseball Day, Nothing Like a Dame Day, and Blah Blah Blah Day.

April 18
According to a Gallup poll, millennials are the least likely generation to belong to a religious institution. The number of people who thought this was news was also at an all-time low.

April 19
The bees living on the roof of Notre Dame Cathedral survived the fire. The beekeeper called it "a miracle." The priests at the cathedral would have preferred a different "miracle."

May 5
Pete Buttigieg went to Sunday school with former President Jimmy Carter at Maranatha Baptist Church. It seems possible that Buttigieg is the first gay-Episcopalian-Harvard graduate-Indiana mayor-Navy veteran to attend a Baptist church in Plains, Georgia.

May 9
Pope Francis released new Vatican laws that clergy members have to report allegations of abuse and attempted cover-ups. The document is titled "Vos estis lux mundi," meaning "You are the light of the world." The laws did not include the phrase "potius sero quam numquam," meaning "better late than never."

May 15

The International Day of Families promotes awareness of issues relating to families. In nations around the world, people explored the 2019 theme: Families and Climate Action. In the United States, Christian families spent the day drinking bottled water, driving everywhere, and cranking up the AC.

May 18

500 million Buddhists celebrated Buddha's birthday. What did Christians give one another for Buddha's birthday? Nothing—which was appropriate.

May 21

University Baptist Church in Waco announced it will allow its ministers to perform same-sex weddings. The church withdrew from the Baptist General Convention of Texas. The only sure things in life are death and bigotry in Texas.

May 25

Baptist Theological Seminary at Richmond graduated twenty-one in its final commencement ceremony. BTSR was the first of fifteen theological institutions to receive funding from the Cooperative Baptist Fellowship. Cynical BTSR graduates wondered if funding five might have made more sense than fifteen.

May 28

In 2018, the Southern Baptist Convention recorded the fewest baptisms in a year since World War II. The record for baptisms was set in 1972. That year—which included the reelection of Richard Nixon and the Christmas bombing of North Vietnam—must have been the most spiritual year in US history.

June 4

Muslims broke their fast at the end of the holy month of Ramadan. Fasting is a spiritual ritual when people reconnect with God, engage in prayer, and study the Quran. Baptist parents explained Ramadan to their children as a month of Vacation Bible School without Oreos.

June 6

Medical debt has become a target for church philanthropy. Pathway Church, in Wichita, Kansas, spent $22,000 to wipe out $2.2 million in debt for 1,600 people. A church member somewhere feared this kind of compassion will keep his church from getting a new sprinkler system.

June 10
The Vatican announced that gender cannot be changed. People whose gender has been changed announced that the Vatican cannot be changed.

June 17
In an effort to strengthen the church in remote Amazon regions where clergy members are scarce, the Vatican is considering allowing older married men to be ordained and assigned there. Many of the women married to men who want to be priests assigned to remote Amazon regions feel that their husbands can serve as single men.

June 19
According to an international survey, roughly seven in ten people say they trust scientists and want to learn more about science and health. Roughly three in ten people should not be surveyed on anything of importance.

June 20
The Supreme Court reversed a lower-court ruling that the forty-foot Maryland Peace Cross, erected to honor fallen soldiers in World War I, is unconstitutional. Justice Ruth Bader Ginsburg, who wrote the dissenting opinion, pointed out, "The cross was never perceived as an appropriate headstone or memorial for Jewish soldiers." Jewish soldiers who fought in World War I were unavailable for comment.

July 8
The Holy Sepulcher in Jerusalem has long been a source of tension between the Christian churches sharing it. The leaders of the Roman Catholic, Greek Orthodox, and Armenian Orthodox churches signed an agreement to renovate the church's sewage system. Some observers consider this a sign of growing cooperation, but custodians do not consider broken toilets a partisan issue.

July 25
During a phone call between President Trump and Ukraine's president, Trump seemed to urge Ukraine to investigate former VP Joe Biden and his son for corruption. On July 28, some clever minister prayed, "God, investigate our hearts for corruption. May your Spirit be our whistleblower."

August 21
President Trump thanked a conspiracy theorist for saying Jews in Israel love the president "like he's the King of Israel" and accused Jewish voters of disloyalty if they vote for Democrats. The King of Israel has not responded.

September 1
A Mississippi venue that canceled a couple's wedding plans after discovering the couple was a black man and a white woman commented, "We don't do gay weddings or mixed race, because of our Christian race—I mean, our Christian belief." Reporters failed to ask what they would have said to Moses and his Ethiopian bride.

September 1
The mayor of Odessa, Texas, blamed video games for the most recent mass shooting. The mayor did not explain why other countries with video games do not have mass shootings.

September 4
Someone drew a circle on a National Hurricane Center map to include Alabama so the president would not have to admit he was wrong. The makers of Sharpies thought this was a good idea.

September 4
Marianne Williamson said, "Millions of people today are praying that Dorian turn away from land, and treating those people with mockery or condescension because they believe it could help is part of how the overly secularized Left has lost lots of voters." Lots of voters continued to treat Marianne Williamson with mockery or condescension.

September 15
The patriarch of the Maronite Church declared thirty-four couples "husbands and wives" in Bkerke, Lebanon. These mass ceremonies minimize the cost of weddings. Fathers of prospective brides across the United States googled "Maronite Church" and "cost of mass weddings."

September 27
Kanye West released *Jesus Is King* to the befuddlement of many. West's portrayal of himself as Jesus with a crown of thorns on the cover of *Rolling Stone* would seem problematic for white evangelicals. His embrace of President Trump makes the African American community skeptical. His self-absorbed persona makes those who care for the marginalized confused.

But West has struck up a friendship with Jerry Falwell Jr., so this could work.

September 27
Pastor Robert Jeffress used the Bible to attack the science of climate change, saying, "Somebody needs to read poor Greta [Thunberg] Genesis Chapter 9 and tell her next time she worries about global warming just look at a rainbow. That's God's promise that the polar ice caps aren't going to melt and flood the world again." The polar ice caps continue to melt.

October 3
Kentucky Governor Matt Bevin is encouraging students to participate in "Bring Your Bible to School Day." In 2017, he signed legislation making Kentucky the first state to allow public schools to offer Bible literacy classes. Sarcastic Ohioans suggested Kentucky observe "Read a Book at School Day" and allow public schools to offer literacy classes.

October 11
Abuse survivor and victims' advocate Rachael Denhollander pointed out that David raped Bathsheba. This surprised people who were unfamiliar with the Bible.

October 15
The Democratic Primary Debate lasted three hours and exceeded 30,000 words, almost none of them about religion. Elizabeth Warren, a Methodist, has repeatedly reflected on her past as a teacher but does not mention that she taught Sunday school. Pete Buttigieg seemed to be the most willing to mention religion on the campaign trail. Southern evangelicals wish someone other than the gay Yankee would acknowledge the importance of faith.

October 23
The Beyoncé Mass, which features black women singers, dancers, and ministers, is a complete church service with a sermon, Scripture readings and the Lord's Supper. White ministers are considering the Bruce Springsteen Mass, the Taylor Swift Mass, and the Garth Brooks Mass.

November 1
Southern Baptist Theological Seminary President Al Mohler tweeted that he is willing to be nominated for president of the Southern Baptist Convention next June. The only people surprised by his willingness to be

nominated were those who thought Mohler was already the president of the Southern Baptist Convention.

November 25
Lawyers for cannabis churches argue that marijuana is a sacrament, but The Sacramental Life Church of Redondo Beach is in trouble with the deputy city attorney, who said, "In the city's opinion this isn't a sacrament of the church. This is clearly a marijuana dispensary. The Catholic church doesn't charge you to drink the wine." Young Baptists were shocked to learn Catholics get real wine.

December 3
Ministers look forward to the year that Giving Tuesday falls on a Sunday.

December 4
North Korea warned the United States of a possible "Christmas gift" if it doesn't meet an end-of-year deadline for concessions. North Korea understands what a real "War on Christmas" would look like.

December 10
House Democrats unveiled two articles of impeachment against President Trump. Trump had two words for all of this: "witch hunt." Trump continues to poll poorly among witches.

December 13
Prime Minister Boris Johnson called today's elections a way to "get Brexit done." The speed with which the UK is leaving the EU makes members of the Cooperative Baptist Fellowship feel better about how long they hung around the Southern Baptist Convention.

What can we expect in 2020? Liberal Christians will continue to vote for Democrats who do not like Christians. Conservative Christians will continue to vote for Republicans who do not think like Christians. The religious movement to address climate change will remain smaller than the religious movement to ignore climate change.

Thoughtful Christians will try to make sense of it all. They will keep trying to be the church, and that should be news.